ART AS SECOND NATURE

Art as Second Nature

Occasional Pieces
1950—74

by
Michael Hamburger

A CARCANET NEW PRESS PUBLICATION

SBN 85635 073 7

First published 1975
by Carcanet New Press Limited
266 Councillor Lane
Cheadle Hulme, Cheadle
Cheshire SK8 5PN

Printed in Great Britain
by W & J Mackay Limited, Chatham

Contents

Prefatory Note

THIS collection was originally advertised as *Selected Essays*. I prefer to call it *Occasional Pieces*, because without exception the contents were produced in response to occasions, as lectures, radio talks, book reviews or other solicited contributions to periodicals. Although they have been selected from a large body of such work done over the years, most of them are not essays in the sense proposed by the opening piece. To call them occasional, as they were, is also to acknowledge a debt of thanks to the begetters of those occasions; and that seems right to me.

Acknowledgements, therefore, are made to the editors of *Agenda*, *Akzente* (Germany), *Chapman* (Edinburgh), *The Christian Science Monitor*, *Dimension* (Austin, Texas), *Encounter*, *Lines Review*, *Neue Rundschau* (Germany), *The Nation*, *The New York Times Book Review*, *Plural* (Mexico), *Poetry Nation*, *The Review*, *The Spectator*, *Stand*, *Studio International* and *World Review*; also to the B.B.C.

Special thanks are due to Professor A. Leslie Willson of the University of Texas and to Professor Alastair Fowler of the University of Edinburgh. 'On "Metrical" Verse, "Free" Verse and Prose' is the post factum text of the Buist Lecture for 1974, delivered from notes at the University of Edinburgh. Its genesis is due as much to the sponsors of that occasion as to the urging of my publisher, Michael Schmidt, to turn it into a script after the event.

M.H.

Part One

Part One

An Essay on the Essay

EVEN that isn't quite right: an essay really ought not to be on anything, to deal with anything, to define anything. An essay is a walk, an excursion, not a business trip. So if the title says 'on' that can only mean that this essay passes over a certain field – but with no intention of surveying it. This field will not be ploughed or cultivated. It will remain a meadow, wild. One walker is interested in wild flowers, another in the view, a third collects insects. Hunting butterflies is permitted. Everything is permitted – everything except the intentions of surveyors, farmers, speculators. And each walker is allowed to report whatever he happens to have observed about the field – even if that was no more than the birds that flew over it, the clouds that have still less to do with it, or only the transmutations of birds or clouds in his own head. But the person who drove there, sat there inside his car and then says he was there is no essayist. That's why the essay is an outmoded genre. ('Form' is what I almost wrote, but the essay is not a form, has no form; it is a game that creates its own rules.)

The essay is just as outmoded as the art of letter-writing, the art of conversation, the art of walking for pleasure. Ever since Montaigne the essay has been highly individualistic, but at the same time it presupposes a society that not only tolerates individualism but enjoys it – a society leisured and cultivated enough to do without information. The whole spirit of essay-writing is contained in the first sentence of the first great collection of English essays – Francis Bacon's of 1597: 'What is *Truth*; said jesting *Pilate*; And would not stay for an Answer.' A jesting Pilate who asks questions but doesn't wait for answers is the archetypal personification of the essay, of essay-writing and essayists. The English essay flourished for three centuries, even when the earnestness of the Victorian age had begun to question its peculiar relation to truth. Only the totalitarian systems of this century turned walking without a purpose into a crime. Since the time of G. K. Chesterton and Virginia Woolf the essay has been a dead genre. Needless to say, people continued – and still continue – to write prose pieces which they call essays; but already George Orwell was too 'committed', too puritanical, too much aware of a crisis to take walks without a bad conscience.

The essay is not a form, but a style above all. Its individualism distinguishes it from pure, absolute or autonomous art. The point of an essay, like its justification and its style, always lies in the author's personality and always leads back to it. The essayist is as little concerned with pure, impersonal art as with his subject. Since the vast majority of so-called critical essays attaches primary importance to subjects, that is, to answers and judgements, the perpetuation of that genre does not prove that the essay has survived. Most critical essays are short treatises. With a genuine essay it makes no difference whether its title refers to a literary theme, whether to the origin of tragedy or the origin of roast pig.

But since the essay is not a form the spirit of essay-writing can assert itself outside the genre. Where confidence in his readership was lacking, for instance, the essayist often changed into an aphorist. Lichtenberg, Friedrich Schlegel and Friedrich Nietzsche were laconic, partly repressed essayists. Essay-writing insinuated itself even into poetry: a pseudo-epic like Byron's *Don Juan* or Heine's *Atta Troll*, whose wit always points back to the personalities of their authors, whose plots are interrupted again and again by their narrators' peripatetic arbitrariness. Story-telling and essay-writing were inseparable in the prose pieces of Robert Walser, and it was no accident that one of them, an outstanding one, was called 'The Walk'. It was the spirit of essay-writing that drove Walser the story-teller into self-destructive parody: 'In Thuringia, at Eisenach if you like, there lived a so-called beetleologist, who once again had a niece. When shall I have done with nieces and the like? Perhaps never. In that case, woe is me! Grievously the girl in the house next door suffered under learned surveillance . . .'

Some of the digressions in Musil's *The Man without Qualities*, too, are genuinely essayistic, because Musil was a seeker, a man without designs who asked questions that he couldn't answer. So are the *Ficciones* of Jorge Luis Borges. So are many of the shorter writings of Ernst Bloch, Walter Benjamin and Th. W. Adorno – however weighty their themes.

The spirit of essay-writing walks on irresistibly, even over the corpse of the essay, and is glimpsed now here, now there, in novels, stories, poems or articles, from time to time in the very parkland of philosophy, formidably walled and strictly guarded though it may seem, the parkland from which it escaped centuries ago to wander about in the wild meadow. But it is never glimpsed where that wild meadow has been banned from human consciousness even as a memory or possibility, where walls have become absolute and walking itself has become a round of compulsion and routine. It has come to terms with the overcrowded streets of large cities, but hardly with factories, barracks, offices, not at all with prison yards and extermination camps. Anyone who can never get these out of his mind cannot tolerate the aimlessness and evasiveness of essay-writing, but calls it shameless, egotistic and insolent. But somewhere or other the spirit of essay-writing is walking on; and no one knows where it will turn up. Perhaps in the essay again, one day?

Music and Words: Beethoven

As a mere listener, I don't feel qualified to contribute to the positive business of interpreting Beethoven's music; but much like a celibate's views on love, my generalizations may have the negative value of provoking those with practical experience. Knowing next to nothing about the technique of music, I have occasionally tried to improve my understanding of a specific work by consulting the written word – interpretations by experts or accounts of the composer's characters and circumstances. Like many literary men, I profoundly mistrust the written word; most of the remarks that follow are the outcome of my struggles with that medium in my endeavours to draw closer to music. And, again like many literary men, I have been particularly fascinated by the late works of Beethoven. My first publishable – and published – poem was written under the influence of part of the B flat Quartet, though no one, I hope and believe, would know it unless he were told.

Unlike literature – and all music criticism is literature, since it uses words – music is pure form and pure consciousness. While we are accustomed to speak of the *content* of a poem or play, to do so in the case of instrumental music is to apply the criteria of literature to an art governed by entirely different laws. The content of a work of music is its form and the feelings – or, better, the states of consciousness – cast into that form by the composer. We have all heard and seen what happens when the authors of programme notes set out to describe a musical work in terms of the emotions it is understood to express or to convey: all we get is inane and irrelevant verbiage. One reason is that what I have called the composer's state of consciousness is something both more vague and more significant than any single emotion: it embraces both thought and feeling, but thought and feeling at the stage where they are neither differentiated nor defined. If the commentator tells us that a certain movement is both melancholy and gay, he may be perfectly right, for the state of consciousness expressed may partake of both these moods, either because it fluctuates between them or because it combines them in a way which only music and great poetry permit. What makes such comments ludicrous is not that they are meaningless, but that ordinary words are incapable of conveying these subtleties. (Another reason, which I cannot elaborate here, is that the emotion expressed and the emotion conveyed are not necessarily identical.) All our attempts to explain the feelings embodied in music must necessarily confine themselves to the crudest generalizations. The only alternative is not to explain them, but to render their equivalent in words; yet the dangers of this course are greater still – for it leads straight to poetic prose of a kind not only inane but embarrassing. This dilemma is strange enough when we consider how successfully words can be set to music: the relationship is not reciprocal, because words are bound to objects and ideas, music only to formal and technical laws. Yet I believe that music can be translated into words; not directly, but by a process of insidious penetration, when the composer's state of consciousness is communicated to the listener and, by a rare coincidence, crystallizes into words. Even in such a case, however, the translation is bound to be extremely free.

Such renderings are the exception; what concerns me here is the common language of interpretation, a language restricted by a crude and general terminology. Take the opening fugue of the C sharp minor Quartet; apart from formal analysis, what can we say about it? We can say it is plaintive or meditative or resigned, that it's a mixture of all these or, with J. W. N. Sullivan, that it contains 'the central experience' of 'the greatest, the most mystical of Beethoven's quartets, the one in which the mystical vision is most perfectly sustained'. But we lack the means of translating a musical theme into the language of thought. Sullivan does not tell us what that mystical vision was, nor can we specify the philosophical theme on which we believe Beethoven to have meditated in that fugue. Writing about another late work of Beethoven's, the great fugue of the B flat Quartet, Sullivan commits himself to the statement that in it 'the experiences of life are seen as the conditions of creation and accepted as such'. But the piece of music itself offers no clue to what Beethoven was accepting, and why; Sullivan can only refer to 'the conditions of creation' because he knows from biographies that the older Beethoven lived for his art – that creation, to him, had become an end in itself. Considered in that light, Sullivan's statement is only another way of telling us that in writing this fugue Beethoven was saying 'yes' rather than 'no': and this, perhaps, is all we can honestly say about the content of what we recognize to be a fugue radically different from any other that has ever been written. The weight and quality of Beethoven's affirmation can be sensed, but not explained.

Now, in the case of a fugue by Bach we should probably be satisfied with a similar piece of information. Not so in the case of Beethoven, and late Beethoven at that; for we know that Beethoven insisted on being called a tone poet, that his late works are not only great music, but that they belong to the class of music which Sullivan described as 'springing from a spiritual context'. We should like nothing more than to know what is *behind* the music, to know more about the vision mentioned by Sullivan or 'the ideas that exist no-where else in music' of which W. J. Turner speaks; but Turner makes it clear from the start that 'nobody can say finally what the later melodies of Beethoven mean'. In fact he goes as far as to claim that 'only a man as great as Beethoven can fully comprehend Beethoven.' Here the non-practising lover of music may be tempted to give up; but wrongly so. I have deliberately chosen to quote writers who were not professional musicians, a scientist and a poet. Turner is confusing two different modes of comprehension – one musical, the other philosophical or literary. Beethoven was a great musician; we have no reason at all to believe that he was a great thinker. As for the greatness of his spirit, it is inseparable from his music, contained in it and contained nowhere else in so pure a form; the question of comprehension, other than musical comprehension, does not arise. Turner makes the mistake of regarding music as a kind of cup into which the composer pours a measurable quantity of greatness: this cup can only be emptied by a person with exactly the same capacity. But greatness is an attribute of the music, not of the man regarded as separate from the music. And all art is a vessel that transforms its contents: what we get out of it may be something greater or smaller than what went in. As I have tried to suggest, what in our loose and literary way we call ideas is not relevant to the appreciation of music; as far as Beethoven was concerned, they are not even relevant to its composition. The ideas that preoccupied him were vaguer than abstractions and more powerful. They were im-pulses: the impulse towards virtue in life and perfection in art, the struggle against fate (and fate was anything that thwarted or afflicted him) and, especially in his later years, the impulse not to despair. This last he called resignation.

Whether or not Beethoven's later music belongs to a category different from the pure music ascribed to Bach – and personally I don't think so – what is certain is that he was never anything so degenerate as a tone poet. His reason for claiming that title is that musicians before his time were regarded as little more than artisans, while poets had long enjoyed a certain modicum of respect; it was Beethoven himself who revolutionized the standing of musicians. But there was no excuse for critics like Paul Bekker, who could conclude his formidable book on Beethoven by stating that 'Beethoven is first of all a poet and thinker, only in the second place a musician'. Nonsense of that kind, though antiquated, still haunts and misleads the ingenuous listener.

If ever there was a man whose first language was music, that man was Beethoven. 'Great thoughts drift through his soul', a visitor reported, 'but he cannot express them in any form but music.' His own letters show that he was often incapable of formulating the simplest thoughts. His most ardent aspirations even were more like impulses than precepts. 'Every day I draw nearer to the goal which I can sense but not describe', he wrote in 1801, and eleven years later: 'Only our striving is infinite'. And it is just the vagueness of his strivings and renunciations that gives them such power to move us in his music, their vagueness that makes them infinite; for the greatest music has no other object than to embody itself in form. We are so much accustomed to the dichotomy of subject and object, feeling and thought, that we have no vocabulary to describe the states of undivided consciousness from which music proceeds; so we resort to talking about it in terms of moods and experiences, emotions and ideas.

The third category of music, according to Sullivan, is programme music; it is music neither pure nor 'springing from a spiritual context'. Beethoven's Pastoral Symphony is sometimes relegated to this class. His sketch-books of the period contain the following notes on the work: 'Pastoral Symphony not a painting but an expression of those sentiments invoked in men by their enjoyment of the country, a work in which some emotions of country life are described . . . Even without a description one will be able to recognize it all, for it is (a record) of sentiments rather than a painting in sounds.' These are not the words of a tone poet, but of a composer very much aware of his limited, but unique medium. Limited, because it cannot describe the visible world or dogmatize about the invisible; unique, because these limitations are a short cut to universal significance.

If even the Pastoral Symphony conveys general, rather than particular impressions of rural life, we have little hope of particularizing the strange inward regions of the last quartets. With the help of formal analysis, we can learn a good deal about their contours, even arrive at certain conclusions as to their character – (Mr Mellers has shown us that form is the surest clue to meaning). Contour maps are no substitute for a living landscape, but they can help us to find our way about. And as far as our musical sensibilities permit, we can enter into those inward regions – by the simple process of listening.

We may or may not believe that the C sharp minor Quartet is mystical, but in either case it remains music – melody, rhythm and harmony – and these call for no special faculty of comprehension. Here again we must beware of being put off by words: for the mysticism – if that is the right word for the states of consciousness expressed in the quartet – is of a kind that has no parallel in literature; at least I know of no mystic whose vision could accommodate the sardonic humour of the Presto movement or the intricate modulations of feeling in the Variations. We are inclined to call mystical what is only mysterious; and often it is only mysterious because it is unfamiliar or difficult. This is not to deny that Beethoven's last works sprang from states of mind never expressed in music before or since; and the better we know them, the more inexhaustible they become. I am only trying to avoid too facile a use of words: for music itself is a mystery, an abstract language that speaks to us more directly than any derived from experience of the concrete world.

But much of the uniqueness of the last quartets (and even of such earlier works as the last four piano sonatas) may well be due to nothing more mysterious than Beethoven's mastery of his medium, a mastery that enabled him to express states of consciousness which strict sonata form could not contain. One thing that distinguished Beethoven from his predecessors was an unusually strong desire to perfect his art, to develop all his individual capacities. 'You must know well enough', he wrote to the poet Matthisson, 'how great a change the lapse of a few years can work in an artist who is always progressing. The greater one's progress in art, the less one is satisfied by one's older works'. And twelve years later, in 1812, to a different correspondent: 'The true artist has no pride; unhappily he sees that art has no bounds. Obscurely he feels how far he is from his aim and, even while others may be admiring him, he mourns his failure to attain that end which his better genius illumines like a distant sun.'

Two and a half years before his death, when he had started work on the last quartets, he confessed: 'It really seems as if I'd scarcely written a note of music'.

Owing, in part, to his deafness, Beethoven's personal development was uncommonly one-sided; the more nearly complete his social isolation became, so did his dedication to music. I believe that the close texture of his last works – and especially of the C sharp minor Quartet, with its delicate transitions from one movement to the next – is intimately connected with his individualism and his one-sidedness. In that extreme isolation the language of music acquired an intensity not otherwise conceivable; and behind every note there is the absolute silence of his deafness. I should hesitate to call it peace; for his development, like his strivings, was infinite. Even the C sharp minor Quartet did not give him the feeling that it had come to an end; in the short time left to him he composed one more quartet and planned at least three other major works.

In a letter of this period he advises Archduke Rudolph to do exercises in counterpoint, and continues: 'Gradually we develop the capacity to express just exactly what we wish to express, what we feel within us . . .' The observation seems commonplace enough; but coming from Beethoven, never more than half-articulate except in music, it amounts to a valuable comment on his late works. Not the least of their characteristics is their unequalled precision, but not the precision of geometrical form; it is the precision of a mastery to which form no longer acts as an obstacle to expression. Because of that mastery, the work is pure inwardness: the impulse and its enactment are one.

On 'Metrical' Verse, 'Free' Verse and Prose

LONG before being told, after a poetry reading at an eminent public school, that only one of the pieces I had read was a poem, all the others were prose – and this not by one of the boys but by the senior English master – I had suspected that there is something wrong with widely held notions of what distinguishes verse from prose, verse from poetry. The piece that had been judged to be a poem was in regular metre, and it had a regular rhyme scheme; all the others were later poems of mine, without end-rhymes and in rhythms not predominantly iambic. Since I had come to this way of writing after a long apprenticeship in metre and rhyme, I found it hard to believe that there could be a difference in kind between my earlier work and the later. (It could well be that in both ways of writing my ear was defective; but my critic had no reservations about the more conventional piece. That led me to wonder whether he had been counting rather than listening.) Many poems of this century that to me are the most musically achieved and authentic are composed in various modes of what most people would call 'free verse'. Yet I am also capable of appreciating verse in what they would call 'regular metres', with or without end-rhymes. I could only conclude that rhythm, in poetry, is something other than metre, and that rhythm is the essential thing; also that, whatever the metre or absence of metre, rhythm is determined more by the distribution of stresses, the speed, weight and length of sound/sense units, than by the correspondence from line to line of a fixed number of 'feet' or syllables. Thus the omission of one unstressed opening beat can turn a whole iambic line into a trochaic one, without a drastic reversal of rhythm if there is no other re-arrangement of stresses in the line.

Leaving aside that 'underground' tradition in English poetry – from experiments by Spenser and Campion to Clough, Doughty, Swinburne, Bridges and Hopkins – which has derived its poetics from attention to accent and quantity, or assonance and alliteration, rather than to syllable-count and end-rhyme – I decided to take a random sampling of excerpts from major English poets, of seemingly regular verse either dramatic or lyrical, to discover what inferences are to be drawn from their practice about the relation of metre to rhythm, and the prevalence or non-prevalence of iambs. No doubt I was as biased towards irregularity as my critic had been towards metre and rhyme schemes. So I must try to meet him on his ground, that of scansion, prepared to count and name the 'feet' I do not believe in.

The rhythmic freedom of Shakespeare's blank verse is so familiar as to need little attesting here. Even in plays of his middle period regular iambic pentameters – containing five stresses preceded by unstressed syllables – are so far from being the rule that one has to look hard for them. In Macbeth's 'Tomorrow and tomorrow' soliloquy – where the special demands of dialogue do not arise – I found one five-stress line: 'Creeps in this petty pace from day to day', but even there the speech rhythm pulls against iambs, calling for reversed 'feet' at the opening and adding an additional half-stress to 'this'. As for

> To the last syllable of recorded time

it is a classic instance of the Shakespearean line that is mimetically right but metrically wrong. A schoolmaster, perhaps, would scan it either:

> Tŏ thē lăst sȳllăble̅ ŏf rĕcordĕd time

or:

> Tō thĕ last sȳllăble̅ ŏf rĕcordĕd time

with one permissible reversal of 'feet' at the beginning, but the ear accepts neither scansion. Both semantically and sonically 'last' demands a stress, making either a spondee – for believers in feet – or an anapest, followed by a dactyl. The syllables scurry away into the dark 'o' of 'recorded'; and so they should, regardless of prosody manuals. Scanned by ear, the line contains two iambs out of the regulation five.

> And then is heard no more. It is a tale

is a regular iambic pentameter only if we disregard that the second 'is' will not support a stress, and that the 'no' compensates *quanti-tively* for the deficient weight of that 'is'. As for 'Signifying nothing', it is an instance of reversal into trochaic rhythm, even if the 'fy' does not obtain a full stress in performance, and the line could still have been made to fall back into iambic if completed.

The blank verse dialogue in Milton's *Samson Agonistes* shows a somewhat greater frequency of regular iambic pentameters, though here, too, the most arresting effects occur where rhythm is most at odds with metre. (The choruses, with their approximation to Greek models and their impromptu rhymes, are a special case.) Only syl-lable-counters will find iambic pentameters in:

> O dark, dark, dark, amid the blaze of noon.
> Irrecoverably dark, total Eclipse
> Without all hope of day!
> O first created beam, and thou great Word,
> Let there be light, and light was over all,
> Why am I thus bereaved thy prime decree?

Rhythmically, this passage is dominated by three-stress clusters – I don't know the technical term for that effect, if it has a name in the manuals – amounting almost to a four-stress cluster, or double spondee, in the opening four words. That accumulation, quantita-tively, weakens the stress on 'mid' to a half-stress at the most, leaving only two true iambs in the line. A similar, though lesser, piling up of stress occurs in 'thou great Word' and again in 'Light was over all', because that 'was', not only phonetically, is an altogether weightier syllable than the 'is' in the *Macbeth* passage.

In Dryden's rhymed couplets I found a marked tendency towards the alternation of irregular pentameters with regular ones:

> Since men, like beasts, each other's prey were made,
> Since trade began and priesthood grew a trade,
> Since realms were formed, none sure so cursed as those
> That madly their own happiness oppose;
> There Heaven itself and godlike kings in vain
> Shower down the manna of a gentle reign.

In the second line irregularity of speech rhythm is set up both by the necessary pause created by the assonance of 'and' with 'be*gan*' and by the relatively weak stress on 'grew'; in the fourth line by the un-certain half-stresses on both 'their' and 'own', then by the weak stress on the 'ess' of 'happiness'; in the sixth line by the virtual spondee 'shower down', compensated by the succession of unstressed syllables between '*man*na' and '*gent*le'. Once again scansion by ear, not counting-machine, bears out the truth of Ezra Pound's remark: 'As to quantity, it is foolish to suppose that we are incapable of distinguishing a long vowel from a short one, or that we are mentally debarred from ascertaining how many consonants intervene between one vowel and the next.'

Even Pope has more irregular pentameters than regular ones in these opening lines of 'Eloisa to Abelard':

> In these deep solitudes and awful cells
> Where heav'nly-pensive Contemplation dwells
> And ever-musing Melancholy reigns;
> What means this tumult in a Vestal's veins?
> Why rove my thoughts beyond this last retreat?
> Why feels my heart its long forgotten heat?
> Yet, yet, I love! – From ABELARD it came,
> And ELOISA yet must kiss the name.

Of these, only the fifth and eighth lines are regular iambic pentameters, unless the first syllable of 'Contemplation' and the third of 'Melancholy' could take fuller stresses in Pope's time than they can now. I am pretty sure that the 'in' of the fourth line never could, semantically; and that no sensible or sensitive reader of any time would, or could, pronounce the two 'yet's of the seventh line as an iamb. Far from being the natural pulse of English verse, the iamb cannot be maintained in the language for long stretches without violating its natural rhythms. The correctness of Dryden and Pope could not change the need for constant variation of stress. Only a pedant could regret this. German iambics tend to much greater regularity. Even the German practitioners of blank verse in the eighteenth and nineteenth centuries appear to have overlooked the precedent of Shakespeare in that regard, producing column after column of iambs that never change step, let alone fall out of it.

That precedent, as well as Milton's, was observed by most of the English Romantics, and I don't intend to pursue the later fortunes of the iambic pentameter. One characteristic Keatsian variant is a line like

In the half-glutted hollows of reef-rocks

in which my ear registers only one iamb, though the full five stresses are there, freely and musically distributed.

*

Yet I shall stay with Keats for a moment, as I turn to more intrinsically lyrical verse forms. His 'La Belle Dame sans Merci' shows an
interesting tension between the seeming iambic norm established
at the outset and the accentual rhythm of popular ballads, which
asserts itself triumphantly with

> And no birds sing,

where a stress-cluster arises from the impossibility of leaving either
'no' or 'birds' unstressed, with the colliding sibilants of 'birds' and
'sing' producing a pause that lends additional weight to those two
words. The three consecutive stresses in four syllables create a
balance of accent, though not of syllable number, with

> Alone and palely loitering –

another three-stress line according to the ear, a four-foot line according to the manuals, which would make another iamb out of the last
two syllables. By the time we reach the second stanza we have
accepted an accentual rhythm that runs counter to the iambic metre
proposed in the opening line.

In the lyrics of both Donne and Herbert a trochaic beat arises as
naturally as an iambic one:

> Goe, and catche a falling starre,
> Get with child a mandrake roote,

and this remains the dominant rhythm despite Donne's notorious
syncopations. Elsewhere, as in 'Twicknam Garden', it is dactyls that
dominate at first, with the open option of any change of rhythm
required by the thematic and emotional dynamics. In 'Twicknam
Garden' iambs take over less than half-way through the second line:

> Blasted with sighs, and surrounded with tears,
> Hither I come to seeke the spring. . .

George Herbert, too – like many English poets – has an instinctive preference for opening his poems with a strong beat. Whether
the dominant rhythm established later will be iambic or not depends
on semantic and kinetic requirements:

> Peace, prattler, do not lowre:
> Not a fair look but thou dost call it foul.
> Not a sweet dish but thou dost call it sowre.
> Musick to thee doth howl.

The exact rhythmic correspondence here between the second and third lines is due as much to a semantic parallelism as to the observance of a metre ostensibly iambic, as the subsequent stanzas show. Sticklers for iambics will question my scansion of 'Not a fair look' and 'Not a sweet dish'. Again, the collision of the 't' of 'sweet' with the 'd' of 'dish', as well as the inescapable weight of both 'fair' and 'sweet', are irrefutable evidence that those words cannot be left unstressed. For Herbert, as for Donne, every iambic metre has to contend with a counter-rhythm more inclined to trochees, spondees and dactyls; and it is this inward counter-rhythm that creates the characteristic tension of the verse. In 'Easter', too, Herbert's strong opening beat breaks his iambic metre even before it is established:

> Rise, heart, Thy Lord is risen; sing His praise.

Where Herbert's metre is trochaic throughout, as in 'Praise', there may be less irregularity.

With William Blake's *Songs of Innocence and Experience* we return to the wholly 'natural' rhythm of English verse, to be found also in popular ballads, nursery rhymes, and any verse composed by ear alone, a rhythm governed by stress and weight of syllables, not by their number:

> 'Father, father, where are you going?
> O do not walk so fast.
> Speak father, speak to your little boy,
> Or else I shall be lost.'

Scanned by an irrelevant metric, the first line is a mixture of trochee and dactyl, the second is iambic, the third a mixture of spondee and dactyl, the fourth iambic. In 'O Rose thou art sick . . .' the mixture is one of iambs with anapests; in 'He who binds to himself a joy . . .', of trochee, dactyl, iamb and spondee. The balance lies in a shifting pattern of stresses and half-stresses, never exactly even in weight, yet sufficiently so to create a strong rhythm.

The long lines of Blake's prophetic poems are as generically and functionally different from the short lines of his lyrics as the epic blank verse of Milton or the dramatic blank verse of Shakespeare is from their lyrics. Yet neither the absence of end-rhymes – even of the half-rhymes allowed by Blake in the lyrics – nor the slightly

greater rhythmic variation amounts to a departure that would make
it meaningful to call the lyrics 'metrical' verse, the prophetic poems
'free' verse. If we count the stresses, not the syllables, Blake's long
lines are often considerably less irregular than the blank verse of
either Shakespeare or Milton.

Then had America been lost, o'erwhelmed by the Atlantic,
And Earth had lost another portion of the infinite.
But all rush together in the night in wrath and raging fire.
The red fires raged! the plagues recoil'd! then roll'd they back with fury
On Albion's Angels: then the Pestilence began in streaks of red
Across the limbs of Albion's Guardian, the spotted plague smote Bristol's,
And the Leprosy London's Spirit, sickening all their bands:
The millions sent up a howl of anguish and threw off their hammered mail,
And cast their swords & spears to earth, & stood a naked multitude –

where the first two lines have five stresses, the remainder seven. The
weighing of stresses, admittedly, is a less mechanical business than
the counting of syllables, involving an element of uncertainty due not
only to the individual reader's ear but to the poet's, as well as to
shifts in the standard accentuation of words and regional peculiarities; but this uncertainty is not confined to verse, like Blake's, that
has shaken off even the pretence of iambulism.

    Whether we read Blake's long lines as 'free' or as accentual verse,
Whitman was far from being the only radical liberator of English
verse in the mid-nineteenth century. Matthew Arnold's 'Epilogue'
has as much rhythmic variety as either Blake or Whitman, though
its predominantly three-stress lines seem to derive from classical
lyrics rather than from epic or biblical models:

>   So I sang; but the Muse,
>   Shaking her head, took the harp –
>   Stern interrupted my strain,
>   Angrily smote the clouds.
>
>   April showers
>   Rush o'er the Yorkshire moors.
>   Stormy, through driving mist,
>   Loom the blurr'd hills; the rain
>   Lashes the newly-made grave.
>
>   Unquiet souls!
>   – In the dark fermentation of earth,

> In the never-idle workshop of nature,
> In the eternal movement,
> Ye shall find yourselves again.

It seems unlikely that Arnold intended a suspended but linking end-rhyme on 'strain', 'rain' and 'again'. In any case the verse requires no rhyme, and the recurrence is so unobtrusive that Arnold's practice here differs in no essential way from that of twentieth-century writers of what most people would call 'vers libre' or 'free verse'. The vocabulary is another matter.

Arnold's 'Rugby Chapel' is a related attempt to get away from both rhymed and iambic verse. One has only to compare his handling of the three-stress accentual line with that of Yeats, who charged it with an altogether fiercer energy – helped by end-rhyme – to realize that Arnold came to this verse form not through Blake or popular verse but through Greek and Latin, so that his experiment is more akin to Tennyson's alcaics or to Clough's hexameters. As in 'Epilogue', the movement is slow, grave, elegiac:

> Coldly, sadly descends
> The autumn evening. The field,
> Strewn with its dank yellow drifts
> Of withered leaves, and the elms
> Fade into dimness apace.
> Silent; – hardly a shout;
> From a few boys late at their play!
> The lights come out in the street,
> In the school-room windows; – but cold,
> Solemn, unlighted, austere . . .

For reasons of diction, again, and especially Arnold's falling back on adjectives and adverbs to convey what rhythm and imagery could convey, and his hesitant syntax does convey without their help, the experiment is not wholly successful; but the poem's hesitations, pauses, rallentando effects point forward to one of the distinctions of twentieth-century 'free verse'.

As for Whitman, the rhythmic structure of his long lines is similar to that of Blake's, except that it is somewhat looser both in variation of stresses per line and the greater frequency of more than the three light or unstressed syllables between stresses which most theorists of English accentual verse considered acceptable to the ear. Where Whitman's verse seems 'prosy', the second of these peculiarities is as likely to be the cause as the demotic turns of phrase that clash with his archaisms. Yet, free or not free, Whitman's verse has the same tendency as any other to establish pattern, correspondences, balance of one sort or another, as in this extract from *Song of Myself*:

I loafe and invite my soul.
I lean and loafe at my ease observing a spear of summer grass.

My tongue, every atom of my blood, form'd from this soil, this air,
Born here of parents born here from parents the same, and their parents
    the same,
I now thirty-seven years old in perfect health begin,
Hoping to cease not till death . . .

a passage consisting of seven-stress lines and three-stress half-lines.

    A related parallelism governs the 'free' verse of T. S. Eliot – no matter whether he liked the relationship or not – though the dominant five-stress rhythm of the opening passage is broken or relieved by short lines gradually diminishing from three stresses to one:

    What seas what shores what grey rocks and what islands
    What water lapping the bow
    And scent of pine and the woodthrush singing through the fog
    What images return
    O my daughter

    Those who sharpen the tooth of the dog, meaning
    Death
    Those who glitter with the glory of the hummingbird, meaning
    Death
    Those who sit in the sty of contentment, meaning
    Death
    Those who suffer the ecstasy of the animals, meaning
    Death

That verse, of course, has a tautness and spareness, as well as a vowel music, quite different from Whitman's. In spite of the tautness, Eliot occasionally allows three or even four unstressed syllables in succession – Bridges considered two the maximum, perhaps because his system is based on 'feet' – as in 'glitter with the glory of the hummingbird' or 'suffer the ecstasy of the animals', and it does seem that the American ear is more tolerant of that effect than the British. Yet Shakespeare had taken the same liberty within the bounds of what is supposed to be an iambic pentameter.

                         *

These pickings and probings could easily be continued well beyond decent book length, extended to the more idiosyncratic byways of English versification, or brought more nearly up to date. The case of Thomas Hardy, whose verse is usually rhymed and seemingly 'metrical' while being essentially improvised, and therefore more free and more rhythmically varied than much of the more modernist verse in part contemporary with it, would confirm what my few random specimens suggest: that the boundary between 'metrical' and 'free' verse, regular and irregular forms, is so vague, so fluid, that these categories tell us next to nothing about the real practice of a poet; also, that the iambic beat – let alone the iambic 'foot' – is no more natural than any other, even if by an accident it established itself in English poetry as a dominant convention.

Whether a poet adopts – and usually adapts – some ready-made framework of metre, or works out his own system of laws and licences depends on the state of poetry in his time and on his peculiar needs at any one stage or moment. In either case he will have to rely on his own ear for the personal rhythm that is indispensable for major work. Where that personal rhythm is lacking no amount of metrical constraint or freedom will make up for its lack. True, 'the facination of what's difficult', of strict or elaborate forms mastered, gives one kind of aesthetic satisfaction; but they are only mastered where the personal rhythm, the 'track of feeling', asserts itself; and since to extemporize with finality and rightness calls for the greatest mastery of all, the strictest or most elaborate forms need not be the most difficult to master.

'True free verse',

Donald Davie wrote in the Autumn–Winter 1972–3 issue of *Agenda*,

> as I have experienced it in the act of writing it, seems bound up with *improvisation*, with 'keeping it going now it has started'. Writing it, you must not be interrupted, and for long stretches you cannot afford to take a break. For this reason I think of free-verse composition as musical, whereas metrical composition lends itself to a steadily punctuated building-up, block by block, architectural: metred verse can go into stanzas; free verse never can.

In music, too, the greatest mastery is shown not in observance of rules – any competent composer can manage that – but in the freedom no composer can afford until all the existing resources of his art are at his finger-tips, the art itself is second nature to him. Bach attained that freedom in counterpoint, as Shakespeare did in blank verse.

Because of the distinction made by Davie, metrical composition is conducive to ingenuity and invention. A regular rhyme scheme, for instance, will inevitably lead the poet to possibilities of meaning or analogy that would not otherwise have occurred to him. It was not until rhyming had become a convention – 'the troublesom and modern bondage of Rimeing', Milton called it – that poets, makers, became troubadors or trouvères, finders. The difference between making and finding is another way of putting Davie's distinction between musical and architectural composition – always bearing in mind that neither distinction is absolute, that in either mode of composition a poet both makes and finds. The purest making, though, excludes all temptation to that virtuosity which calls attention to itself. In pure making 'the poetry does not matter', as Eliot wrote; or, to go back to Horace and back beyond the rhyming convention, the 'art lies in the concealment of art'.

Regularity and irregularity of form, then, are not in themselves valid criteria in distinguishing verse from prose, or good verse from bad verse. 'If a man has no emotional energy, no impulse, it is of course much easier to make something which looks like "verse" by virtue of having a given number of syllables, or even of accents, per line, than for him to invent a music or rhythm-structure. Hence the prevalence of "regular" metric. Hence also bad "vers libre".' Those few words by Ezra Pound sum up the whole complex.

As for the prose poem – to which French writers might never have resorted at all if they had not been driven to it by the tyranny of their academic prosodists – it is by no means the same thing as free verse or 'vers libre'. Poems in prose, as Baudelaire called them, combine the density of poetic utterance with the rhythms of prose. Many would-be poems in free verse are prose poems chopped up into lines; but so are many would-be poems in regular metres, if their rhythm is mechanical, inorganic, and unrelated to what the poem sets out to enact. In English, prose poetry has most often served for anecdote, fable, or extended epigram, though longer works, like those of David Jones or Samuel Beckett, can also be regarded as prose poems; in French, more often for flights of vision and imagination that would be cramped by the rhythmic restrictions of verse, even of 'vers libre'. Poetry calls for a high degree of reduction – of theme, gesture and movement – to which all its complexities must be subordinated. Where such reduction is prohibited by the subject matter, prose is the better medium; for prose can digest more poetry than poetry can digest prose. If the prose poem, or piece of imaginative prose that is not a short story or novel, were more widely recognized and accepted as a valid genre, we might be spared much intellectually demanding verse that raises expectations which it cannot fulfil, having bitten off more prose material than it can chew.

Recurrence, correspondence, symmetry offer the surest and most primitive guarantee of cohesion in a work of art; but the greater a poet's mastery, the more variation and modulation of rhythm he or she can afford. Since freedom is the hardest discipline of all, one constant danger at present is that poets will overrate their own capacity for rhythmic improvisation; another, that they will resort to inorganic pseudo-forms, useful to them as a substitute for traditional metres, but useless to their readers because no real cohesion or urgency has been transmitted. 'Syllabic verse' is a case in point – metre divorced from rhythm; a less blatant one, the practice of squeezing blocks of lines that have no unity of movement, gesture or theme into symmetrical frames – as though fourteen lines necessarily amounted to a sonnet, or a stringing together of such arbitrary chunks amounted to a sequence. In both cases a numerical principle of production has been mistaken for the process of composition; or Donald Davie's 'musical' improvisation confused with an 'architectural' building up.

What makes a piece of verse 'prosy' is not irregularity but slackness of rhythm. In that sense 'free' verse that is poetry is not free – as Eliot suggested; and metrically regular verse that is rhythmically slack is not poetry either. Scansion, at best, confirms what the ear knew all along.

Art as Second Nature: Goethe

I

IT is difficult to think of a more refractory subject for a new biography than Goethe. To begin with, no writer's life has been more thoroughly and minutely documented, so that a biographer is confronted with a mass of disparate material far too great to be compressed into a single book intended for the general reader. The problem of selection and emphasis is exacerbated by the nature of Goethe's 'life and times'. Goethe, notoriously, was 'protean', his interests, activities and literary works were incomparably many-sided, and his times extended from the old order in Europe to the French Revolution, the Napoleonic wars, the post-Napoleonic restoration and the new revolutions of 1830. As for Goethe's connection with all these successive eras, it is as enigmatic and ambiguous as everything else about him. On the one hand, Goethe was closely in touch with the makers and victims of history, and the *Zeitgeist* is evident enough in a few of his earlier works; on the other hand, he became curiously impervious to current issues, so much so that not only his later works, but his later life, can be seen as a bulwark raised against the violent upheavals of the age. Marxist critics like Professor Hans Mayer are not alone in regretting this development, which they regard as a kind of betrayal of Goethe's early allegiances and as an unfortunate precedent for the 'non-political' stance of later German writers.

Goethe was also the first poet to be conscious of the revolution which, for a century or so, elevated imaginative writers, artists and composers to the status of heroes, sages and 'representative men'. If he could not foresee the extraordinary process of re-interpretation by which he was turned into a national, cultural and educational institution after his death, he himself made quite sure that posterity should know more about him than about any writer before hi   Yet he was equally careful to keep this public image both enigmatic and ambiguous: the 'fragments of his great confession' – shored not so much against his ruins as against the erosive petty-mindedness of

later generations – were decidedly of his own choosing; and even the
unprecedented industry of his biographers and biographically minded
critics has not succeeded in establishing many more facts about his
love affairs, for instance, than he was prepared to divulge.

Goethe's most recent biographer* has overcome most of the
special difficulties which his subject poses. He has omitted few of the
known facts of Goethe's life compatible with the scale of his book,
and his account of Goethe's times is outstandingly well informed.
He has no axe of his own to grind, but the very matter-of-factness of
his presentation, his reluctance to speculate or only to comment at
length, and his refusal to indulge in hero-worship, do amount to a
re-appraisal of Goethe. Though far from deliberately debunking
Goethe as Lytton Strachey debunked the great Victorians, Dr Friedenthal's study is cool and searching enough to have upset a good
many of Goethe's German admirers. The 'Olympian' of legend is
shown to have been very human in his fear of death, sickness and
disorder; his outward serenity to have been maintained at the cost
of callousness towards the sufferings and misfortunes of others. All
this is not new. Goethe himself confessed that he had rarely been
happy, and that too much of his life had been wasted on activities
marginal to his true vocation. His apparent coldness, egoism and indifference had struck many visitors to Weimar. It is Dr Friedenthal's
treatment of Goethe's works, or the balance between his treatment
of Goethe's works and his treatment of the 'life and times', that does
less than justice to Goethe.

An occasional paraphrase of a line or two of verse and a few
summaries of plots are simply not enough to convey the vaguest idea
of Goethe's achievement as a writer, far less to trace the subtle inter-
connections between his works and his life, his works and his times,
the multiplicity of his media and the single mind that informed them
all. What is more, some of the English renderings are utterly misleading. The famous lines from *Tasso*

> Und wenn der Mensch in seiner Qual verstummt,
> Gab mir ein Gott zu sagen, was ich leide

are one shocking example. The translation, 'and when a man is
speechless in his pain, there is a God to help him tell his agony' is
not only bad blank verse, but bad prose, since it manages to obscure

* Richard Friedenthal, *Goethe: His Life and Times*, Weidenfeld & Nicolson
London, 1965.

the crucial difference between the 'me' of these lines – Tasso – and other men, so that the whole quotation becomes pointless.

A masterly short poem written in Goethe's old age is described as follows:

> To these observations he adds a *Lebenslied*, a song of midnight the sound of whose bells has accompanied him from childhood to the fullness of his manhood. Musingly he repeats the dark-sounding word 'midnight' at the end of each stanza; it is a warning of a last midnight that now draws near.

The poem 'Um Mitternacht' – and one must assume that this is the poem in question – contains no such warning. On the contrary, it expresses a far more characteristically Goethean joy in a morphological process that has not only linked his end to his beginning, but blessed his old age with a new freedom and mastery, a lightness and litheness enacted in the colloquial diction, informal syntax and improvised structure of that very poem:

> Um Mitternacht ging ich, nicht eben gerne,
> Klein, kleiner Knabe, jenen Kirchhof hin
> Zu Vaters Haus, des Pfarrers; Stern am Sterne,
> Sie leuchteten doch alle gar zu schön;
>   Um Mitternacht.
>
> Wenn ich dann ferner in des Lebens Weite,
> Zur Liebsten musste, musste, weil sie zog,
> Gestirn und Nordschein über mir im Streite,
> Ich gehend, kommend Seligkeiten sog;
>   Um Mitternacht.
>
> Bis dann zuletzt des vollen Mondes Helle
> So klar und deutlich mir ins Finstere drang,
> Auch der Gedanke willig, sinnig, schnelle
> Sich ums Vergangne wie ums Künftige schlang;
>   Um Mitternacht.
>
>
> At midnight, far from gladly at that hour,
> A small, small boy along the churchyard I
> Walked to my father's vicarage; star on star,
> O how they shone, too richly lit the sky;
>   At midnight.

When later I, moved farther though not far,
Must see the loved one, must because she drew me,
Above me stars and northern lights at war,
Going and coming I felt bliss flow through me;
    At midnight.

Until at last the full moon made a rift
So bright, so clear within the dark of me,
And even thought, grown willing, limber, swift
Embraced both past and future easily;
    At midnight.

The description, clearly, does not fit the poem; nor does it give the slightest indication of its distinction – of the way, for instance, in which the imagery of light renders a progression that is essential to the whole of Goethe's work, including his scientific and critical writings. A similar kind of progression or 'Steigerung' – to use Goethe's term – has been discovered even in the very much earlier, and seemingly simple, 'Wanderers Nachtlied' beginning 'Über allen Gipfeln'. Professor E. M. Wilkinson* has shown how the images in that song render 'an order of the inner processes of nature as known by the mind, an organic order of the progression in nature, from the inanimate to the animate, from the mineral, through the vegetable, to the animal kingdom, from the hill-tops, to the tree-tops, to the birds, and so at last to man.' It would be grossly unfair to expect Dr Friedenthal to have engaged in textual analysis of this sort in a book that is not a work of literary criticism, but his misleading description of the late poem brings one up against the limitations of his very medium, the literary biography, as well as against a certain glibness that could have been avoided even in a biography remarkable for its pace, compactness and readability. If Goethe is judged more by his life than by his works, he is likely to appear as a dilettante or – as T. S. Eliot at one time saw him – as a man who 'dabbled in both philosophy and poetry and made no great success of either'. The deplorable wrongness of that view – which T. S. Eliot corrected on a later occasion – makes it imperative for readers of this biography to refer to Goethe's own works and to such critical studies as the excellent essays by Professors Willoughby and Wilkinson. Many of Goethe's works are not easily available in English translation, but

*E. M. Wilkinson and L. A. Willoughby, *Goethe: Poet and Thinker*. Edward Arnold London, 1962.

his range as a lyrical poet is fully represented in Dr F. D. Luke's selection in the Penguin Poets series.

II

That very range, it is true, can easily puzzle and disturb an un-prepared reader; and the sheer quantity of Goethe's published works – not to mention the even larger body of secondary literature that has accumulated around them – is such as to discourage anyone who is not prepared to devote his whole life to their study. Here a know-ledge of Goethe's 'life and times', including the kind of summary of Goethe's activities which Dr Friedenthal provides, is an indispensable aid. Not only Goethe's personality, but his historical situation too, was full of contradictions. A general awareness of that situation makes it much easier to appreciate the unprecedented character of Goethe's universality.

The Germans regard Goethe as a classical writer, as their classical writer *par excellence*. To his earlier English critics he was a romantic. Since Goethe's works cut through these categories, as they cut through almost any other, it is important to redefine the terms in the light of Goethe's situation. Above all, one must distinguish between a disposition and a mode. It was Schiller who remarked on the 'naivety' of Goethe's genius and on his deep kinship with the ancient Greeks. Yet in another sense no writer can be classical in an age of social and artistic revolutions. Goethe could function as a classical writer in those of his works which he wrote for the diminutive and obsolescent aristocratic society of Weimar – in his entertainments, libretti, occasional public verse and the like. Those of his works, on the other hand, which are close imitations of ancient models are not classical in that sense, but classicizing. They are very modern in their deliberate resort to a norm not given but looked for; and in many ways Goethe's situation is comparable to that of modern poets like T. S. Eliot and Ezra Pound, with their carefully selected inter-national canons of exemplary works, later equivalents of Goethe's *Weltliteratur*. One reason for the diversity of Goethe's forms and media is that the models available to him were already so various as to approximate to the modern *musée imaginaire*; they ranged from native folk song to Renaissance Italy and France, from late medieval Germany to ancient Greece and Rome, and on as far as Persia, India and China.

The greater the range, the greater the need for a centre, if only for a centre that must remain partly invisible, cryptic and personal. Hence Goethe's need not only to 'dabble' centrifugally in so many things, but to be independent, uncommitted, elusive. As Dr Friedenthal writes:

> . . . the minister and *Geheimrat* are roles in Goethe's life, but they are minor roles. Much of his activity was mere bustling about, evasion of more difficult tasks, or relaxing after his creative periods. Much that he did should have been left to others. He had no particular gift for organization; he was unable even to organize his own household properly. A born ruler, he was at the same time lazy and quick to show impatience. Detail, on which he set so much store, bored him and was left to subordinates. In keeping with his dual nature, however, he would sometimes meddle with extraordinary obduracy in petty details, and till his very last days there are countless documents and memoranda that bear his signature. The essence of the matter is contained once and for all in the letter he wrote to the Duke on his return from Italy: 'Accept me as a guest, at your side let me fill to overflowing the measure of my existence . . .'

Socially, too, Goethe's situation was not as simple as it has been made out to be, for instance by Thomas Mann, who celebrated Goethe as a 'representative of the bourgeois era'. That bourgeois era – of which Thomas Mann was a late representative – had scarcely begun in Germany when Goethe was active. Before Weimar, Goethe was identified with the revolutionary *Sturm und Drang*, a movement less bourgeois than working-class. Despite his own middle-class background, Goethe's affinities always veered between the nobility and the 'common people'. Weimar society, in fact, was strikingly deficient in an affluent, self-assured bourgeoisie; with the single exception of the enterprising 'capitalist' Bertuch, its bourgeoisie was powerless and depressed. Goethe's notorious indifference in later years to political and social issues has a great deal to do with his isolation in an era not yet bourgeois as far as the greater part of Germany was concerned, his growing awareness that he was writing only for a few 'kindred spirits', the 'happy few' to whom Stendhal also addressed himself. Much of the edition of his collected works issued from 1787 to 1790 remained unsold for more than a century; and mint copies of the first edition of the *West-Östlicher Divan* – a work essentially unpopular and esoteric – could still be found in bookshops as late as the First World War. By then, of course, the new nationalistic or liberal bourgeoisie had done its utmost to appropriate and digest this elusive poet; but it is important to note that even his immediately popular 'bourgeois epic' *Hermann und Dorothea* is set in a Germany still untouched by the industrial revolution.

As Dr Friedenthal stresses, Goethe remained a 'wanderer' and an exile even when he was rich and famous, no longer living as the favourite and minister of a prince, but more like a prince in his own right. He had devoted enough time and hard work to the administration of a tiny, backward and ultimately powerless State to have become incapable of attaching a more than symbolic importance to the business of government. Realist though he was in many regards, Goethe was ultimately concerned with the realities of nature, including human nature, rather than with the changing realities of politics and society. He respected these, but looked beyond them, with an increasingly Platonic concentration on essences and universal laws. That is why in literature, too, he could make use of so many conventions, without being wholly contained within any one of them. The playfulness of his old age – seemingly contradicted by the stiff formality that was his defence against intruders – presupposes a seriousness and a commitment to which nothing was wholly trivial, irrelevant or alien, because everything was related to an immutable centre. Where that relation is not apparent to us, it is the triviality and irrelevance that make us uncomfortable.

III

With no dominant tradition, no national culture and no clearly defined public to rely on, Goethe was not only the last 'Renaissance' or all-round man, but also the first of the moderns. About the often evasive sage of the late Weimar period, after his escape to Italy and virtual retirement into private life, there is an almost Joycean aura of 'silence, exile and cunning'. Goethe knew how much of his later fame was due to the appeal of *Götz von Berlichingen* and *Werther*, works which he had long outgrown, how little to what he had become after his liberation in Italy. Against that misunderstanding he adopted the defence of 'egoism'; but before airing our moral indignation we should consider the extent to which Goethe's ego was a vehicle for something other than himself – for nature, or – in terms of Groddeck's psychology – for the It. Goethe's 'dilettantism', his

refusal to force himself into a single mould or will himself to produce
this or that kind of work, was inseparable from his unique openness,
his unique faith in the rightness of nature, his unique readiness 'to be
lived', as Groddeck puts it, and perpetually transformed. Schiller,
the man of theories and ambitions, sensed all this when he remarked
on Goethe's rare capacity to reap without having appeared to sow.
'I had come to the point of thinking of my indwelling poetic talent
as Nature pure and simple', Goethe himself wrote in his autobiography; and, in the context of a defence of Ovid in the same work,
'I tried to maintain that the productions of an outstanding individual
are themselves products of nature.'

Goethe's faith in nature and his sense of being a favoured vehicle
of nature were strangely 'presumptuous', as he himself admitted,
but the completion of *Faust* shortly before his death, and after more
than half a century of allowing the work to grow, amply vindicates
that presumption. Nor is the presumption as egoistic as it seems.
'Who am I?', Goethe asked in his extreme old age. 'What have I
created? I have taken and absorbed everything that I have heard and
observed. My works have been nourished by thousands of the most
diverse natures, fools and wise men, clear heads and dullards. My
work is that of a composite being, and it bears the name Goethe.'
His lines addressed to 'original' people convey the same recognition:

> Vom Vater hab ich die Statur,
> Des Lebens ernstes Führen,
> Vom Mütterchen die Frohnatur
> Und Lust zu fabulireen.
> Urahnherr war der Schönsten hold,
> Das spukt so hin und wieder;
> Urahnfrau liebte Schmuck und Gold,
> Das zuckt wohl durch die Glieder.
> Sind nun die Elemente nicht
> Aus dem Komplex zu trennen,
> Was ist denn an dem ganzen Wicht
> Original zu nennen?

> My build from Father I inherit,
> His neat and serious ways:
> Combined with Mother's cheerful spirit,
> Her love of telling stories.
> Great-grandfather courted the loveliest,
> His ghost won't leave me alone;

> Great-grandmother liked fine jewels best,
> This twitch I've also known.
> If, then, no mortal chemist can
> Divide the components from the whole,
> What is there in the entire man
> You could call original?

This brings one back not only to Goethe's 'pagan' reliance on nature, but also to his modernity. The reference to Groddeck's 'It' becomes less far-fetched* in view of the late Goethe's freedom from prejudice in sexual matters – his cheerful allusions to homosexuality, for instance, in the *Venetian Epigrams* and even at the end of the second part of *Faust*, or his candid examination of temporary impotence in the verse diary rightly included in Dr Luke's selection. Goethe could be anachronistically shameless in such matters because he saw the shameless It at work where his contemporaries saw only the precious, responsible, original ego. This does not mean that Goethe had no use for morality or decorum. He hated unbalance, monomania and disorder. In his art criticism he went so far as to censure landscape painters who did not maintain a proper balance between images of growth and images of ruin or decay. He rejected the morbid one-sidedness of much Romantic literature and art.

One of his greatest achievements in prose, the late, allegorical *Novelle*, is full of delicate allusions to an unmistakably Goethean sense of propriety. The extreme formality of its manner – eminently civilized and deliberate, unlike the rhapsodic nature-worship of his *Sturm und Drang* – spans all the many strata that must divide human society from animal nature; yet the same distance is also bridged in that story, the eighteenth-century antinomy of Art and Nature is reconciled, and a wild beast tamed by the music and trustfulness of a child. This late work is a true microcosm of the old writer's mind, rich in experience of the most diverse realities, yet reaching out beyond appearances to a higher, still unrealized plane of meaning. Nature, to Goethe, extended to the conscious mind; his faith in nature was not an atavistic rejection of intellect or will, but a recognition that even intellect and will are related to nature, and

---

* When writing this I had not realized that Groddeck's 'It' derived from his early reading of none other than Goethe! This became clear only in the collection of Groddeck's miscellaneous essays *Psychoanalytische Schriften zur Literatur und Kunst* published by Limes Verlag, Wiesbaden, in 1964. See especially pp. 26, 32 and 43.

that 'the whole man must move at once' if he is to evolve, to be 'intensified'.

Even Goethe's 'reactionary' antagonism to Newton's optics or to the microscope is at least understandable in view of what specialization has done to the world. Any part that could not be fitted into the whole was apt to be impatiently dismissed by Goethe – morbidly 'subjective' talents in the arts as much as atomizing, de-humanizing trends in the natural sciences. This impatience marks the limits of Goethe's power to absorb and synthesize. That there should have been such limits is no more astonishing than Goethe's personal shortcomings and failures. Every reader of *Faust* knows that error, remorse and perplexity have their place in Goethe's religion of growth. 'In life – all is metamorphosis', he said to S. Boisserée in 1815, 'with plants and with animals, right up to and including man'; or, put the other way round, 'metamorphosis is all.'

On Anonymity

THE pros and cons of anonymous criticism continue to be debated from time to time. However, since there are very few prominent periodicals left that insist on the principle of anonymity, in practice the discussion tends to revolve around a single periodical, the *T.L.S.*, as far as literary criticism is concerned. In this special case the continued insistence on anonymity has to do with the circumstance that the weekly is, or at least originated as, a supplement – and as a supplement to the newspaper that prided itself more than any other on being representative, impartial and comprehensive. New books, too, were to be reported, above all, like news items. If it wasn't possible to exclude criticism, that is, value judgements – and the very selection of books reviewed rests on value judgements – at least the judgements were to be as representative, impartial and comprehensive as possible. Whether anonymity ever served to create more than the semblance of a true impersonality, is very doubtful; but, in Great Britain at least, it was easier fifty years ago than it is now to find a large number of contributors capable of conforming to a common style and at least appearing to constitute a body of opinion. Certain standards – not only aesthetic but ethical and social – were still valid for the majority of potential contributors despite their specialized interests and fields of study. *The Times Literary Supplement* was written by gentlemen for gentlemen (and, of course, ladies). That in itself made for a measure of agreement, even in the matter of style.

At least the semblance of unanimity could be maintained, as well as an authority due to this semblance, in as much as readers were given the impression that here books were not judged by fallible individuals but by a literary tribunal. British statesmen and politicians are still apt to refer to themselves in public speeches or interviews not as 'I' but as 'one', as though by this grammatical shift they could rid themselves of the tiresome and unnecessary condition of being individuals, with the danger of immodesty, and so of indecency, entailed in that condition. Anonymous critical contributions also prohibit the use of the first person, which in the *T.L.S.* has to be circumscribed as 'your reviewer' or 'this reader', though more often it is replaced by the same apparently impersonal 'one'. This is not to deny that many of its current contributors do their best to subordinate their personal prejudices, vanity and preferences, if not their personal judgement, to a general decorum; but the nature of this decorum is no longer self-evident. Even the nature of a gentleman is no longer self-evident; and neither all the statesmen and politicians nor all the writers and readers of the *T.L.S.* in contemporary Britain necessarily want to be regarded as gentlemen.

Perhaps anonymity would still be justified if it could be relied upon to prevent a critic from consciously or unconsciously falling into partisanship, or from using criticism as a pretext for an exhibition of his cleverness and originality. But, to judge by my experience, individuality and vanity are so deep-rooted that anonymity cannot even conceal them, let alone annul them. Several contributors to the *T.L.S.* can be recognized by their manner; several by their point of view; several by their specialization; a few by their malice, their stupidity or their narrow-mindedness. Smugness is another characteristic which an editor can no more keep out of the columns than he can those others I have named. This leakage in anonymity may not affect the majority of readers, who are indifferent to the identity of contributors. But every intelligent and experienced reader of criticism is aware that the proper understanding of a critical piece demands some knowledge of the critic – at least in an imperfect world, and as long as no individual can reduce himself to a plain 'one' without drastic and unusual metamorphoses. That's why I am in favour of an undisguised, uncamouflaged, shameless 'I' – though of an 'I' that does its best to be fair, doesn't take itself too seriously, and recognizes to what degree every so-called 'I' in turn consists of a 'One' or 'It'.

I do accept the ideal advantages of anonymity. But if the *T.L.S.*, compared with other periodicals, still strikes one as representative, impartial and comprehensive this has less to do with anonymity than with the circumstance that in Britain literature has not been as thoroughly politicized as in other Western countries, not to mention the East European. In West Germany, for instance, the publication of almost any work of imaginative literature has become a political event – or no event at all. In Britain one does not expect the literary columns of any weekly or daily paper to accord with its political line.

It is obvious enough that despite anonymity the most various political opinions and points of view are represented in the *T.L.S.* But because these different voices are hidden behind the mask of anonymity the whole burden of responsibility falls on the editors – just as it does in the case of incompetent or irresponsible reviews of works far too specialized for the editors to be in a position to exercise their judgement. Without the safety valve of readers' letters this state of affairs would probably have become intolerable long ago. Yet again it isn't due to anonymity that reviews in the *T.L.S.* so often give rise to impassioned and amusing correspondence. Rather it is due to anonymity that in such correspondence the reviewer sometimes enjoys an unfair advantage over authors or other correspondents, both because he is protected by his anonymity and because he tends to be given the last word. At the worst, then, anonymity can become a refuge for irresponsible reviewers.

That the authors of outstanding contributions may remain unknown could be construed as an advantage of anonymity – at least by a moralist repelled by the vanity of writers. Yet it is difficult to believe that a writer less vain than the next man is the one most likely to be corrupted by being named – especially in a country where neither authors nor critics are pampered by the kind of prestige that endangers character. (A much more common cause of deterioration in a critic is the sheer routine of reviewing.) In any case, the *T.L.S.* does publish special articles that are signed; and many of the more distinguished ones that appeared there anonymously are reprinted in books by their authors. As far as I know, no one has yet argued that such a breach of anonymity is harmful to the periodical, the critic, or the public.

Its outward clinging to the institution of anonymity has not prevented the *T.L.S.* from being pretty thoroughly modernized in other respects, such as its openness to developments in the arts that have not been noticed at all in other literary periodicals. At the same time it can still offer contributions that remind one of the period when it was founded. This discrepancy may be representative, too, in that it corresponds to general tensions, but it also makes readers all the more curious to know the identity of contributors, so that they can make the necessary allowances. A literary tribunal doesn't contradict itself; so these columns must be written by fallible, imperfect individuals; and what is said or written by fallible, imperfect individuals can be properly understood only if one knows who those individuals are. This may be regrettable in view of the theoretic advantages of anonymity; but there is no getting away from it in practice.

A measure of objectivity, fairness, disinterestedness – all the ideal advantages of anonymity can be attained without that game of hide and seek. A man can say 'I' and still be modest, if not humble. I can say 'one' and not only mean 'I' but attribute an importance to that concealed 'I' which it doesn't deserve. Indeed, an arrogance that pretends to impersonality is more seductive and more dangerous, if only because it's less likely to make one laugh. The decisive thing about anonymity is who and what are behind it.

Existential Psycho-analysis

As long ago as 1931 a Freudian psycho-analyst, Dr René Laforgue, made Baudelaire the subject of a long and thorough-going study, so that we are familiar with Baudelaire the sadist, Baudelaire the masochist, Baudelaire the mother-fixated, Baudelaire the fetichist, Baudelaire the *voyeur*; in short, a Baudelaire endowed with an interesting range of perversions, as well as with impotence.

M. Jean-Paul Sartre's *Baudelaire* could be less embarrassing to squeamish readers who have not yet come to terms with Freud – if there are such readers still; but it is incomparably more destructive than any Freudian analysis could possibly be of the poet who, after all, wanted to be 'before all else, a great man and a saint', if only in his own eyes. Sartre's attack is more formidable because it seems to penetrate to the essential Baudelaire, the individual and the artist. The Freudian libido is a thing so universal and impersonal that a poet's reputation can easily survive the orthodox prying of psycho-analysis. Whatever monstrosities may be brought to light – and Baudelaire himself can hardly be said to have shrunk from monstrosities – we can be sure that these will not account for a poet's ability to write good verse. An Oedipus complex is at least as common a complaint as indigestion. A decidedly pre-Freudian and eminently classical poet, Dryden, was not ashamed to record that he would purge himself before getting down to work: 'When I have a grand design, I ever take physic and let blood; for when you would have pure swiftness of thought and fiery flights of fancy, you must have a care of the pensive part: in fine, you must purge the belly!' All that psycho-analysis has done is to shift the 'pensive part' – which even in Dryden's day also included the emotive part – a little lower down the body. The innovation hardly calls for the hue and cry that has been raised against it.

Sartre's main argument is that 'men always have the kind of lives they deserve'. Though the generalization is a dubious one, it makes sense in relation to Baudelaire, most of whose afflictions were not obviously or directly due to outward circumstances beyond his control. Baudelaire was a suitable subject for Sartre's form of analysis because – to a most unusual degree – he was, and knew that he was, what Sartre claims that all men are, solitary and free. Being free, men are responsible only to themselves, and this responsibility entails choice. Baudelaire, Sartre argues, had an ambivalent attitude to freedom. More aware of it than most people, he was afraid of it and did his best to put off the moment of choice. He took care to remain dependent on his mother, his step-father and his guardians; and, instead of resorting to 'a wider and more fruitful ethic which he should have invented himself', he accepted an established ethical code that condemned him. He wanted to be judged and condemned, so as to escape from his responsibility and his freedom. 'He was the man who felt most deeply his condition as a man, but tried most passionately to hide it from himself.'

Referring to the resolutions that Baudelaire made during the crisis of 1862 and at other periods of his life, Sartre writes:

> They were simply a system of rigid and strictly negative defences. Sobriety meant not taking intoxicants: chastity – not going back to those young women who gave him too kindly a welcome and whose names are preserved in his notebook; work – not putting off until tomorrow what could be done today; charity – not being irritable or bitter and not being indifferent to other people.

If these resolutions are 'negative defences', so is any ethical resolution that demands a restraint of impulses recognized to be harmful either to others or to oneself. What Sartre condemns as negative is not a resolution that could, in fact, have saved Baudelaire, but the ethical values on which it rested; and the alternative, a Nietzschean or Gidean immoralism, was among the possibilities envisaged by Baudelaire himself, but rejected as being of little use to him.

Another way in which Baudelaire is claimed to have evaded the necessity of choice was to turn himself into an object, to divide himself into two persons, one of whom was called upon to judge the other. 'Baudelaire was the man who chose to look upon himself as though he were another person; his life is simply the story of the failure of this attempt.' The super-ego is a familiar concept in Freudian psychology – not to mention anything as old-fashioned as a conscience. But Sartre invests the functioning of this part of Baudelaire's psyche with a special metaphysical significance by

connecting it with his favourite terms, 'existence', 'being', 'consciousness' (*existence pour-soi*), 'non-consciousness' (*existence en-soi*),
'freedom', 'responsibility' and 'choice'. 'Because he wanted at the
same time to be and to exist', he writes of Baudelaire, 'because he
continually fled from existence to being and from being to existence,
he was nothing but a gaping wound.'

Again and again in Sartre's analysis Baudelaire is reduced to being
only this or that – a gaping wound, at this juncture, just as his life
was '*simply* the failure to look upon himself as another person'. It is
true that even Sartre has to concede some greatness and nobility to
Baudelaire at another point, because 'flabbiness, abandonment and
slackness seemed to Baudelaire to be unforgivable sins'; and Sartre
is certainly indebted to that peculiarity of his subject, since it
provides him with the evidence needed for his experiment in existential psycho-analysis, evidence that Baudelaire was ready to provide
because he knew that in the last resort he would be judged by his
works, not by the wretchedness of his life. What is more, Sartre
asks us to remember that 'man is never anything but an imposture' –
another typical reduction, but so sweeping that it does rather palliate
what he writes about Baudelaire, while making one unphilosophical
reader wonder how a man who claims no divine illumination, and
does not believe in it, can pronounce his own species to be an
imposture.

In fact, what is left of Baudelaire after an autopsy that includes
Freudian probings of Baudelaire's perversions, narcissism, exhibitionism and impotence, but goes beyond them to the existential
core, is less mangled than one might have feared. Some of Sartre's
discoveries do seem to reflect on Baudelaire's poetry, as when he
writes:

> If we could put out of our minds the exaggerated vocabulary which
> Baudelaire used to describe himself, forget words like 'frightful',
> 'nightmare' and 'horror', which occur on every page of the *Fleurs du
> Mal*, and penetrate right into his heart, we should perhaps find beneath
> the anguish, the remorse and the vibrating nerves something gentler
> and much more intolerable than the most painful of ills – Indifference.

We might, indeed, as well as those ills that Baudelaire was apt to
render in the somewhat garish vocabulary of late Romanticism; but
once again it is Baudelaire's lucidity and truthfulness to which
Sartre owes the evidence. Baudelaire himself noted: 'Life has but

one charm, the charm of gambling. But what if we are indifferent to gain or loss?' That remark even anticipates some of Sartre's philosophical premises, such as the statement in this very book that 'Life is nothing more than a game; man has to choose his own end without waiting for orders, notice or advice' – except that Baudelaire is more wary of generalizations and prescriptions.

It is the last sentence of Sartre's study that brings out the difference between the analyst and the analysed, the philosopher and the poet:

> Baudelaire was an experiment in a closed vase, something like the *homunculus* in the Second Part of *Faust*; and the quasi-abstract circumstances of the experiment enabled him to bear witness with unequalled éclat to this truth – the free choice which a man makes of himself is completely identified with what is called his destiny.

This final reduction of Baudelaire to an experiment gives Sartre's game away. Elsewhere Sartre has set out to prove that his existentialism is a humanism; but to reduce the life of any man, regardless of whether he was 'great' or 'noble' – as even this post-mortem allows Baudelaire to have been – to an experiment conducted for the sole purpose of validating a theory not even held by that man is to diminish, if not to deny, the man's humanity. It is Sartre who has created the 'quasi-abstract' circumstances of the experiment and placed Baudelaire in a closed vase. Baudelaire, as his many self-contradictions show, was a man aware of countless possibilities, and of his freedom to choose between them. The only substantial condemnation that Sartre has added to Baudelaire's self-condemnations is that Baudelaire's ethical choice was different from Sartre's; and that condemnation, too, raises grave doubts about Sartre's own humanism, his own use of the words 'choice' and 'freedom'.

The processes of poetry are more pragmatic, and less arrogant, than those of existential psycho-analysis. So are the processes of Freud's tentative writings on art and literature.

Psycho-analysis and Art*

OF the many kinds of readers who will be interested in this journal, my kind may well be the most peripheral, since I am not a psychologist or even a literary Freudian. It is to these that Lou Andreas-Salomé's record of the inner circle's transactions in 1912 and 1913 will prove indispensable for what they reveal not only about Freud's personality and opinions, but also about the schisms of those years, the secession of men like Adler, Jung and Stekel. As a privileged member of the inner circle – Freud would address his remarks to her and twice commented on the disturbing effect on him of her empty chair – Lou was allowed to attend the lectures and discussions in Adler's group, and indeed she testifies repeatedly to Freud's tolerance and openness to correction even in these critical years. Her summaries of the papers read and discussed in both groups are crucial to the history of psycho-analysis; but, as Professor Leavy observes, they lack the lucidity of Freud's own writings, and this will limit their appeal to non-specialists. Lou came to psychology from literature and philosophy, not from clinical research or medical practice; it is ideas that continued to fascinate her, for all her interest in specific cases and her scepticism towards the 'premature syntheses' of which she accuses revisionists like Jung. Her fervent admiration for Freud – whom she calls 'heroic' and contrasts with Jung, whose 'earnestness is composed of pure aggression, ambition, and intellectual brutality' – owes much not only to Freud's fitness as a father figure, but to the attraction of opposites. It is almost in mystical terms that Lou sums up her debt to Freud and psychoanalysis in the brief 'Conclusion'; her tone and style are the very opposite of Freud's.

Yet it is the continuity and consistency of Lou's preoccupations that strike and intrigue a non-Freudian reader like myself. As Lou makes quite clear, Freud's 'heroism' lay in his honesty, in an in-

* *The Freud Journals of Lou Andreas-Salomé*, translated with an Introduction by Stanley A. Leavy, Basic Books, 1964.

tellectual radicalism that braved every kind of opposition; and that same honesty had attracted Lou to Nietzsche some thirty years earlier, even if Nietzsche's honesty came to grief through insufficient self-knowledge. Only Freud made this self-knowledge possible, though Nietzsche's intuitions and insights had come close to it at times. Freud, therefore, held the key both to Lou's self-knowledge and to her understanding of a whole succession of personal relationships, including that with Nietzsche, as well as current relationships with Rilke, her husband, and other men. That is why she could write in the 'Conclusion' that, thanks to psycho-analysis, 'all the vanished persons of the past arise anew, whom one has sinned against by letting them go; they are there as from all eternity, marked by eternity – peaceful, monumental, and one with being itself . . .'

It is the non-Freudian in me, however, that feels uncomfortable when Nietzsche is described as 'that sado-masochist unto himself' – as though Nietzsche's quarrel with himself could be explained by that neat and stereotyped label – or when Rilke, who is still Lou's friend, if not her lover, is described as 'a typical hysteric' and compared with another of Lou's lovers, 'a no less typical obsessional neurotic bound up in a thousand reproaches and fixations'. This kind of 'detachment' points not so much to Lou's self-knowledge – she is somewhat more discreet about her own neuroses – as to her narcissistic exploitation of men from the very beginning, whether for intellectual stimulus, physical satisfaction – or psychological investigation, as in these instances. Lou's interest in narcissism comes out not in self-analyses, but in general and theoretical speculations scattered through the journal. Somehow it seems to me that the same delicacy or discretion might have been extended to men like Rilke, who has suffered more than enough from the posthumous revelations of his friends. Lou adds details about his physical ailments, as well as a sympathetic and valuable account of his state of mind in 1913, when 'his production has become fragmentary'.

Yet Lou was well aware that 'in his case the only index of these things is to be found in his creative work'. Like Freud himself, she was prepared to make every sort of allowance for the exceptional problems of exceptional men and women. Lou records this very important admission by Freud:

> It appeared that the world is indeed less in need of improvement and less capable of it than one might think. One finds types whose socially harmful instincts have developed in such intimate union with their

most valuable ones, that one might at best strive only for a better distribution of the forces than that which took place in their childhood. Or conversely those types in which one sees not so much the neurotic patient as a neurotic world; they would need only courage to attain their natural development within their unnatural milieu, but with it they would destroy this milieu too.

To Lou, this was an instance of Freud's weariness and pessimism; to me, it is an instance of his wisdom, his constant awareness that many things are beyond the reach of psycho-analysis. Lou herself was always ready to admit that certain Freudian concepts were still too crude and undifferentiated to be generally effective in diagnosis or treatment; but she was less ready than Freud to dispense with the consolations of dogmatism. As Nietzsche knew, it takes strength to doubt, as well as to believe.

Lou is at her best, and at her least turgid, when she does speak from personal experience, as in her analysis and justification of infidelity in erotic relationships, or her frequent disquisitions on the psychology of women. Professor Leavy rightly points out that Lou's feminism was quite different from the more widespread sort that stresses the equality of the sexes. Her experience of Nietzsche and other intellectually outstanding men – not including Freud – had rather tended to confirm her belief in the emotional superiority of women, if not in the superiority of the emotions to the intellect. This is one reason why she was attracted to Nietzsche's irrationalism and Rilke's 'bisexual' inwardness before her discovery of the Freudian unconscious. 'We must realize that man can never have suffered more fundamentally than in becoming a conscious being,' she comments on the concept of the libido in Freud, Jung and Ferenczi, 'seeing the abyss plunging between himself and the rest, between his race and the world, the beginning of the inner-outer division.' This division was Lou's, as it was Nietzsche's and Rilke's, and this is where her philosophical and literary concerns link up with the psychological, and psycho-analysis itself links up with philosophical and literary developments going back the best part of three centuries. Even Lou's passing remark on schizophrenia, which she sees as the 'wish to be the whole, to be All', touches in the most illuminating way on this central dilemma of modern western man. One does not need to be a Freudian to appreciate Freud's heroic confrontation of it, or to find much that is relevant and engrossing in Lou Andreas-Salomé's book.

A Refusal to Review Kierkegaard*

To review this book is indecent, like giving a running commentary on the eruption of a volcano, from a safe distance. But even this excuse was forestalled by Kierkegaard himself in the journals:

> When I die, there will be something for professors! These wretched rascals! And it does not help, it does not help in the least, even if it is printed and read over and over again. The professors will still make a profit of me, they will lecture away, perhaps with the additional remark that the peculiarity of this man is that he cannot be lectured about.

Kierkegaard's journals cannot be reviewed because they are not a piece of literature, nor a contribution to philosophy, theology or any other of our snug categories. Kierkegaard despised literary elegance as he despised both poets and scholars, and as for priests, theologians and philosophers, he castigated them throughout the journals as so many hypocrites and parasites. As a piece of literature, these last journals are full of flaws, being disjointed and repetitive despite the careful editing and selecting done by Professor Gregor Smith. Yet to read them is to be ashamed of one's demands for tidiness and coherence. The only thing that mattered to Kierkegaard in these last years was the urgency of his discovery of what it means to be a Christian, together with the related task of exposing the sham and 'twaddle' of Christendom.

What Kierkegaard demands of his reader is nothing less than a definite and decisive 'Either-Or'. Short of that there is nothing to be said about these journals. To quibble with this or that statement, to tell the volcano off for being too violent, too extreme, is merely to evade the decision and admit to oneself that this book has passed one by.

* *The Last Years: Journals 1853–55*, Søren Kierkegaard, edited and translated by Ronald Gregor Smith, Collins, London, 1965.

Briefly, Kierkegaard's message is that Christendom, or official Christianity, is a travesty and a mockery of Christ's teaching, because being a Christian means 'dying to the world', means sacrifice, torment and solitude, and 'the New Testament is intended . . . to wound the natural man in the severest possible way.' In Holy Scripture, he says, 'those whom God has loved are always unhappy'. In Christendom, on the other hand, 'the divine blessing has descended on all the trifles and philistinism'; the pursuit of worldly ambitions, the raising of a family, connubial love, money-making, and the indulgence of every vanity have been made compatible with calling oneself a Christian. To Kierkegaard, even the pursuit of knowledge is vanity and 'science is a distraction'. That is why he prefers cannibals to priests and professors, and writes that 'anyone who wants to understand human life as a whole would do best to study the criminal world – this is the really reliable analogy.' For reasons partly personal – and in Kierkegaard, as in Nietzsche, personal reasons are not only as good, but better, than any other – he reserves a special contempt for the press and for journalists, because they foist opinions on a body of readers, and so prevent those readers from becoming individuals. 'If I were a father and had a daughter who was seduced,' he notes, 'I should by no means give her up; but if I had a son who became a journalist I should regard him as lost.'

Kierkegaard's hatred of the natural man – who is also the social man taking refuge in the herd from his true condition – could be mistaken for misanthropy, but for repeated reminders whose sincerity is as patent as the sincerity of every word in this book:

> Ah, it is with sorrow that I write this. In melancholy sympathy, though myself unhappy, I loved men and the mass of men. Their bestial conduct towards me compelled me, in order to endure it, to have more and more to do with God.
>
> So the result has been that I have undeniably come to know what Christianity is; but this truth gives me pain.

His attitude to women will give even more offence though he is equally honest about his later immunity to seduction:

> And strangely enough, wherever they get it from – presumably from instinct – women seem to suspect that so far as I am concerned, just when they make the greatest efforts I would burst out laughing – and no woman will risk this at any price.

Alas, there is some truth in this, that it could end with my bursting out laughing. But the reason is neither my great virtue nor my great spirituality but – my melancholy.

It is on a psychological insight, too, that Kierkegaard based his reservations as to the fitness of women to become Christians in his sense, to experience God as the absurd, and to become 'immense egoists' for the sake of spiritual truth:

. . . It is my testimony as a psychologist that no woman is able to endure a dialectical reduplication, and everything Christian has a dialectical element in it.

To be able to be related to the Christian task it is necessary to be a man, a man's hardness and strength are required to be able to bear just the stress of the task.

A good which is recognized by the evil it brings; a salvation which is recognized by its making me unhappy; a grace which is recognizable by suffering, and so on – all such things (and all Christian things are such) can be borne by no woman, she would go out of her senses if she had to be stretched in such a tension.

As for children, it is of course sheer nonsense that they should be Christians.

The reason, however, is not any intellectual superiority of men over women and children, for faith, according to Kierkegaard, 'tends to the will and personality, not to intellectuality'; hence his dismissal of all the rational arguments that have been adduced for the existence of God, his impatience with scholastic theology and the priests and professors. The only proof of the existence and nature of God is an existential and experiential one; and Kierkegaard stresses again and again that he can offer no more than his own experience:

I must continually emphasize that I do not call myself a Christian. My task is to set the problem, the first condition for the possibility of speaking about Christianity . . .

. . . I am not an apostle bringing something from God with authority.

No, I am serving God, but without authority. My task is to make room for God to come.

So it is easy to see why I must be quite literally a single man, and so must be maintained in great weakness and fragility . . .

The *Journals*, therefore, are not so much edifying, as profoundly shocking and disturbing, since they call in question not only official

Christianity of every kind, but the humanistic and materialistic values, including the aesthetic and artistic, that have replaced religion, as Kierkegaard knew that they would. His critique of Christendom includes a critique of paganism and Judaism, which to him was a form of paganism, because 'every existence in which life's tension is resolved within this life is Judaism', and that precisely is what Christendom, as distinct from Christianity, enabled men to do. The very last entry in these journals, written a week before his death, sums up the very uncomfortable message that Kierkegaard offered in place of the blessings and palliatives of official religion:

> The definition of this life is to be brought to the highest degree of disgust with life.
> He who is brought to this point and can then hold fast, or he whom God helps to hold fast, that it is God who out of love has brought him to this point – he it is who from the Christian standpoint has passed the examination of life, and is ripe for eternity . . .

I must withhold comment on this message, since all the comment I could provide has been anticipated and forestalled in the book, and described in advance as chatter, tittle-tattle and twaddle. Nor should it be necessary to add that Kierkegaard's was one of the finest and purest minds in the whole history of literature – which he despised, like all history – and that it is a privilege to be in the presence of such a mind.

A Writer on His Work: 'At Fifty-five'

Country dances
Bird calls
The breathing of leaves after thunder –
And now fugues.
Modulations 'impolite'
Syncopations 'unnatural'.
No more clapping of hands
When moonshine had opened their tear-ducts
Or fanfares clenched
Heroic nerves –
But a shaking of heads:
Can't help it, our decomposer,
Can't hear his own blundering discords.

As if one needed ears
For anything but chitchat about the weather,
Exchange of solicitude, malice –
And birdsong, true, the grosser, the bouncing rhythms.
Uncommunicative? Yes. Unable
'Like beginners to learn from nightingales'.
Unwilling, too, for that matter –
To perform, to rehearse, to repeat,
To take in, to give back.

In time out of time, in the concert no longer concerted.
But the music all there, what music,
Where from –
Water that wells from gravel washed clean by water.
All there – inaudible thrushes
Outsinging the nightingales, peasants
Dancing weightless, without their shoes –
Where from, by what virtue? None.

By what grace but still being here, growing older?
The water cleansed by gravel washed clean by water.

Fugue, ever itself –
And ever growing,
Gathering up – itself,
Plunging – into itself,
Rising – out of itself,
Fathoming – only itself
To end, not to end its flowing –
No longer itself –
In a stillness that never was.

This poem was written in September 1964, and it surprised me for
several reasons. The dramatic monologue or *persona* is a kind of poem
which I had written in my late teens and early twenties, but never in
the fifteen years or so which preceded the writing of 'At Fifty-five'.
It is a poem about music, or more specifically about a composer of
music, Beethoven, and this too did not fit in with my conscious preoccupations in 1964. It was in 1950 and 1951 that I had been im-
mersed in Beethoven's work and personality, for at that time I was
editing and translating a collection of his letters, journals and con-
versations. I had even dabbled in music criticism at that time,
without any other qualification than a special concern with the
relationship between music and words, music and literature; but this
concern, I thought, was a thing of the past.

Poems know better. One of the great rewards and delights of
writing poetry is that poems tell one what one is thinking and feeling,
what one is and has been and will be, where one has come from and
where one is going. There was a time when I thought that I knew
what I believe, and I imposed this knowledge on the poems I wrote.
These are the poems which now embarrass me. The ones that don't
embarrass me are the ones that surprise me, because they know more
than I do – even about myself.

'At Fifty-five' is not about myself – not about my circumstantial
self, at any rate, or about the self that entertains conscious beliefs and
thinks it knows what kind of poems it ought to be writing at any
particular time. Yet in a different way, which is difficult to explain,
every thing and every person one writes about in poetry is part of
oneself. Though I may wonder why I wrote a *persona* poem at the
age of forty, or why this *persona* was Beethoven, I am also sure that

this poem had to be written as and when it was written – perhaps because the connections traced in it between Beethoven's earlier and later music correspond to something that was happening to me.

In its metrical freedom 'At Fifty-five' is closest to the very earliest monologue I had published, the poem 'Hölderlin', written at the age of seventeen; and the later poem contains a line borrowed from Hölderlin, 'Like beginners to learn from nightingales'. In the meantime, for twenty years or so, I had written mainly formal and metrically regular verse, including sonnets and rhymed songs. In an obvious, too obvious, sense, this verse had 'aspired to the condition of music'. It took me a long time to rediscover metrical freedom and a different, more subdued, more hesitant music. The contrast between Beethoven's symphonies and his late piano and chamber music had always fascinated me. Now it seemed to have a bearing on my explorations and discoveries; and, despite all the fundamental differences between music and poetry, I was struck by the possibility that some music and some poetry could be alike in aspiring to the condition of silence.

All these suggestions as to what the poem is about are vague, tentative and incomplete. Beethoven's deafness is another subject or theme of the poem, and his deafness is linked with changes both in his work and in his outer life, as well as with the refinement of his inner ear. Memory is touched upon, as a faculty midway between experience and imagination; and there are allusions to the more active part which memory plays in the compositions of artists who have passed into middle age, or beyond it. The first lines refer to Beethoven's Sixth Symphony – with its approximations to programme music – and the fugue of the last lines represents the other end of Beethoven's range, a form at once 'pure' and – in his case – highly personal. Only a 'stream of consciousness' poem could have spanned the distance between those seeming opposites, and further comment on them would offer only a specious resolution of the conflict between them.

In his extant utterances Beethoven showed little awareness of the differences between his early and later music. The poem, therefore, does not draw on a single statement by Beethoven himself. Yet neither is it a statement of my own position or creed. Direct observation of nature, not excluding human nature, is far from being dispensable to me as a poet, as it may seem to be to the Beethoven of this poem. One of my recent poems, written in America, hinges on the call of a bird previously unknown to me, the chickadee. In relation to nightingales, as in relation to Beethoven's art, I remain a beginner, with any amount to learn from all that I hear and see.

What, then, does the poem state? It makes no assertion at all. It enacts a process. And as far as I am concerned it matters little whether the person of a poem is my own or another man's, whether the poem records what I have seen and heard or what I imagine another man to have seen and heard. The subject of a poem is the most deceptive thing about it. It is the subject beneath the subject that gives an underlying unity to one's work as a whole, however various and disparate the occasions to which the titles point. This subject beneath the subject is beyond the poet's control. It is only by re-reading his work, or reading other people's responses to it, that he becomes aware of the continuity.

'At Fifty-five' says something about music, but it isn't music criticism. It says something about Beethoven, but it isn't biography It says something about myself, but it isn't a confession or profession. The poem knows better than I do what it's about, what form it must take, what material it needs.

Outside poetry I make decisions and choices, commit myself to one course of action or another, assert my moral judgement and preferences. In poetry my personal will is overruled, my judgement subordinated to the poem's demands. This may be what Keats meant by 'negative capability', and what has long made poetry suspect to those – the great majority in any age – who read it not to be surprised, but to be confirmed in what they know and believe. Such readers want an unambiguous message or narrative line. But the poetry is in the tension and ambiguities. 'Out of the quarrel with ourselves we make poetry', Yeats said; and the true readers of poetry, too, are those prepared to quarrel with themselves, to lose themselves in order to find themselves, to be temporarily disconcerted before recomposing themselves.

Those two musical terms remind me that in poetry all orders of experiences are interchangeable, so that poetry – however specialized in itself – remains a sure antidote to specialization. The language of poetry is at least as precise as good prose, but its precision serves a different purpose. The right word in prose hits the nail on the head. The right word in poetry drops like a stone into water, making the sense spread out in a widening circle. That is one reason why the poet's person or 'I' matters so little. He may use the first person and mean anyone. He may use the impersonal 'we' and mean himself, failing to make the circle widen. Outside his poems a poet may be – and usually is – an egotist; inside them he feels his ego dissolve, intermingle with all that he names or invokes.

Part Two

Hölderlin

THE uniqueness of Friedrich Hölderlin is more obvious than his affinities with other German writers of his time. His mature work – that written between 1796 and 1804 – belongs neither to Weimar Classicism nor to any of the phases and varieties of German Romanticism. After his apprentice work, under the tutelage first of Klopstock, then of Schiller, Hölderlin went his own way, a way more essentially solitary than that of any other poet of his age, with the possible exception of William Blake. Yet one historical approach to Hölderlin is through certain basic antinomies common to all the major German writers of his time. Ancient and modern, naive and sentimental (in Schiller's peculiar sense of 'sentimentalisch'), Nature and Art – these are the most crucial of the antinomies with which Hölderlin was as deeply, and dialectically, involved as his immediate predecessors and his contemporaries, not excluding the philosophers. To the last, that is, until the breakdown of his intellectual faculties in his mid-thirties, Hölderlin grappled with those antinomies, both in his theoretical writings and in his practice as a poet. The intensity of that struggle has a great deal to do with the prodigious speed and extent of Hölderlin's development within the short period granted to him for mature work. Those who saw Hölderlin only as an inspired visionary – as the *sacer vates* only, rather than the *poeta doctus* – failed to notice his extraordinary capacity for self-criticism and for critical reflection on his own work. As his essays and letters show, Hölderlin repeatedly questioned, modified or even rejected the premisses of his art. That is the main reason why his *Empedocles* – a tragedy originally conceived in neo-classical or classicist terms – remained unfinished, as did the Pindaric hymn 'Wie wenn am Feiertage . . .'. In his *Hölderlin-Studien* Peter Szondi traced the connection between the non-completion of those works and Hölderlin's new insights into the nature of ancient and modern poetry. The same insights that caused Hölderlin to abandon certain of his works drove him on to new modes and possibilities of poetic utterance so daring as to anticipate the stylistic innovations of the late nineteenth and early twentieth centuries.

This aspect of Hölderlin's achievement needs to be stressed because of the persistence of a view of him that attributes more importance to his madness than to his artistry and his intellectual power. Nothing could be more wrong, for instance, than W. H. Auden's pronouncement: 'Translation also favours poets like Hölderlin and Smart, who were dotty, for their dislocation of normal processes of thinking are the result of their dottiness not their language, and sound equally surprising in any . . .' Mr Auden went on to contrast these dotty poets with others 'whose principal concern is with the sound of words and their metrical and rhythmical relations'. Hölderlin's principal concern as a poet was with precisely those things; even his characteristic dislocation of conventional syntax in his late poems was based on discoveries about the structure of ancient poetry. Nor was Hölderlin ever 'dotty'; when his very considerable intellectual powers declined, so did his technical inventiveness and his stylistic innovations.

What Hölderlin struggled for, in fact, was not uniqueness or originality – though his work is highly original and unique – but a 'rightness', a balance between ideas of perfection derived from Winckelmann's neo-classicism and what he called 'life' – vitality, dynamism and immediacy. Something of that balance was attained even in his early classical odes, as compared with the rhymed 'hymns' that preceded them, with their idealistic impetus always in danger of losing itself in abstraction; but the balance was relatively easy to attain within the narrow scope of brief odes that are little more than epigrams. From these brief odes of 1797 onwards – through the longer odes to the elegies, hexameters and free verse hymns – all Hölderlin's subsequent development was in the direction of concreteness, of 'life' – yet without any loss of idealism or of vision. His early epigram about the 'descriptive poets' who 'report all the facts' remained valid for him even when his poetry had arrived at a sensuous vividness of imagery unparalleled in the poetry of his time. A number of these late poems and fragments point forward to W. C. Williams's 'no idea but in things'. Yet Hölderlin never aspired to realism for realism's sake. The more esoteric and intensely personal his vision, the more difficult it became to strike the right balance between the general and the particular, pathos or 'drunkenness', as he called it, and the sobriety and measure that were equally dear to him.

The capacity for self-criticism on which I have remarked is apparent even in the poems themselves, from the brief odes to the free verse hymns. In 'Menschenbeifall' ('Human Applause') he comments on the change between his prolix Schillerian verse and the spareness of his new medium:

> Has love not hallowed, filled with new life my heart,
>   With lovelier life? Then why did you prize me more
>   When I was proud and wild and frantic,
>   Lavish of words, yet in substance empty?

In another ode of the same year, 'An die Jungen Dichter' ('To the Young Poets') he formulates that balance between the great antinomies of the age which he was to exhaust himself in perpetually adjusting and redressing in the light of new experience, of new and more ambitious endeavours:

> Quite soon, dear brothers, perhaps our art,
>   So long in youth-like ferment, will now mature
>   To beauty's plenitude, to stillness;
>   Only be pious, like Grecian poets!
>
> Of mortal men think kindly, but love the gods!
>   Loathe drunkenness like frost! Don't describe or teach!
>   And if you fear your master's bluntness,
>   Go to great Nature, let her advise you!

Into the eight sober lines of this seemingly didactic or admonitory poem Hölderlin has packed any number of seeming contradictions, contradictions that give life to the poem because they are part of Hölderlin's quarrel not with others, but with himself. To begin with, the seemingly didactic nature of the poem is contradicted by the injunction not to teach. The Winckelmannian 'Stille der Schönheit' (not rendered literally in my English version, which transposes Hölderlin's Asclepiadean ode into more amenable Alcaics) is corrected, if not contradicted, by the final reference to the authority of Nature – with the implication that imitation of the Greeks is not enough. Yet neither is Nature to be imitated, in the naturalistic sense of description. Drunkenness and frost, excessive enthusiasm and academic perfection, are placed at either end of a single prohibition, so that the half-line in itself creates a balance between them. Piety toward the Greeks is distinguished from a piety like that of the Greeks, with implications pointing both to Hölderlin's fervent pantheism at this period, a pantheism most explicit in his novel *Hyperion*, and to a whole line of argument extending from Lessing through Herder, Goethe and Schiller to the early works of Friedrich Schlegel. The dialectical structure of Hölderlin's works, including *Hyperion*, is more apparent in some of the longer odes, with their clear progression from thesis to antithesis and synthesis; but these few random observations may help to indicate some of the tensions contained within so small and relatively unambitious a poem.

In these brief odes of 1796, then, Hölderlin establishes one kind of balance, and defines it in terms still more general than particular. The distinction of these poems is that their diction and cadences enact and exemplify what is said in them, so that mere epigram is transcended; what these poems lack, on the other hand, is the tragic intensity of the longer odes, in which the clash of opposites becomes ever more extreme and more dynamic, the imagery more concrete, the syntax more true to the tensions which it serves to convey. This development from poem to poem cannot be traced here; it would require analyses not only of the odes, and of subsequent versions of the same odes, such as the many later odes that are like variations on themes first stated in the short odes of 1797, but also of the elegies and free verse hymns. Hölderlin's prodigious development must be followed in the poems themselves, in the three successive versions of the *Empedocles* tragedy, and in his essays and letters. Up to 1804, the letters and theoretical writings confirm, Hölderlin never ceased to reconsider the questions and antinomies most vital to him and to his poetry, and there is an intimate connection between the changes in his theological and philosophical position and the changes in his poetic practice. Nor did he cease to comment on his own poetic practice even in poems as impersonal and oracular as the late hymns, as when he interrupts the celebration of Christ in 'Der Einzige' ('The Only One') to confess:

> For this time too much
> From my own heart the song
> Has come; if other songs follow
> I'll make amends for the fault.
> Much though I wish to, never
> I strike the right measure. But
> A god knows when it comes, what I wish for, the best.

True, this poem – in the first version quoted here – remained a
fragment, and its fragmentary state, like that of the earlier hymn
'Wie wenn am Feiertage . . .' testifies to one of several crises and
conflicts so extreme as to leave the poet temporarily unbalanced. The
'right measure', as he says, evades him here, though he was indeed
to restore it, to establish it anew, in related poems like 'Patmos'.

Hölderlin's development as a whole can be grasped only through
the antinomies with which he struggled until they consumed him,
turning into impersonal myths like those of his very last odes,
'Ganymede' and 'Chiron', or of the free verse fragments which he
published together with them as *Nachtgesänge*. Already in an earlier
ode the antinomy between Nature and Art had been mythologized
in terms of the antagonism between Saturn and Jupiter, in such a
way as to link up with an even earlier ode 'Der Zeitgeist'. The
divided allegiance, in the late poems, between Christ and the Greek
gods progresses from, but does not nullify, the terms of that earlier
conflict. Where a conflict cannot be resolved within a single poem,
the resolution is often suspended until new, purely poetic resources
have made it possible for Hölderlin at once to recapitulate and
transform it. In such cases he was compelled to evolve new poetic
forms, if not a new kind of poetry. Thus in the ode form alone he
was able to encompass epigram, pure lyric, tragic conflict and
catharsis, and even epic, as in 'Stimme des Volks' ('Voice of the
People'). That he was critically aware of these possibilities is proved
by his theoretical reflections on the interaction of lyrical, tragic and
epic elements within all poetry, whatever its dominant mode or
kind.

The opening section of Hölderlin's elegy 'Brod und Wein' ('Bread
and Wine') was highly admired in his lifetime; Clemens Brentano
praised it, treated it as a separate poem, and in that way gave credit
to Hölderlin for excelling even in a mode which he never cultivated
for its own sake:

Round us the town is at rest; the street, in pale lamplight, grows quiet
    And, their torches ablaze, coaches rush through and away.
People go home to rest, replete with the day and its pleasures,
    There to weigh up in their heads, pensive, the gain and the loss,
Finding the balance good; stripped bare now of grapes and of flowers,
    As of their hand-made goods, quiet the market stalls lie.
But faint music of strings comes drifting from gardens; it could be
    Someone in love who plays there, could be a man all alone

Thinking of distant friends, the days of his youth; and the fountains,
  Ever welling and new, plash amid fragrance from beds.
Church-bells ring; every stroke hangs still in the quivering half-light
  And the watchman calls out, mindful, no less, of the hour.
Now a breeze rises too and ruffles the crests of the coppice,
  Look, and in secret our globe's shadowy image, the moon,
Slowly is rising too; and Night, the fantastical, comes now
  Full of stars and, I think, little concerned about us,
Night, the astonishing, there, the stranger to all that is human,
  Over the mountain-tops mournful and gleaming draws on.

In that opening section Hölderlin comes close to descriptive verse, though to a description evocative enough to satisfy a Romantic sensibility. Yet the realism of the townscape here has a special function within the context and structure of the whole elegy, and already in the closing lines of this section a delicate transition prepares us for the cosmological and chiliastic significance of Night. The realism, therefore, serves only to establish one pole of a tension that runs through the whole elegy, a tension between the particular and the general. The diction of the elegy, now elevated and sublime, now starkly colloquial (as in the lines questioning the usefulness of poets in Hölderlin's own time) enacts the same tension. As in all Hölderlin's mature work, it is the antinomies that impose the peculiar rightness and balance to be achieved. That opening section does not contradict Hölderlin's reservations about descriptive poetry; but it shows a progression to a stage where description, too, had its place among the resources available to him as a poet.

At a still later stage, shortly before his mental collapse, he was able to dispense not only with regular form and metre, but also with similes and other rhetorical devices of traditional poetry. The tensions now could be entrusted to images and to the relationships between them created by a syntax no longer governed by the laws of discursive logic. The best-known, though by no means the only instance of this later practice, is 'Hälfte des Lebens' ('The Middle of Life'):

> With yellow pears the land
> And full of wild roses
> Hangs down into the lake,
> You lovely swans,
> And drunk with kisses
> You dip your heads
> Into the hallowed, the sober water.

But oh, where shall I find
When winter comes, the flowers, and where
The sunshine
And shade of the earth?
The walls loom
Speechless and cold, in the wind
Weathercocks clatter.

Of such fragments – and 'Hälfte des Lebens' was a fragment of a
longer poem until Hölderlin had the genius and daring to publish it
as a poem complete in itself – Christopher Middleton has written:
'Hölderlin's later imagery is the crystal lava of his unique and
perilous inspiration . . . What makes Hölderlin's later work sing is
the marvellous balance of energy between disintegration and articu-
lation, plus the mortal conflict of spirit that is going on between these
poles.' Even here, then, there was conflict and balance – on the very
verge of incurable madness.

Büchner's *Danton's Death*

EVERYTHING that is known about Georg Büchner's first play is so extraordinary as to defeat every explanation in terms of cause and effect, historical trends or personal development. It was written in 1835 by a twenty-one-year-old medical student with no experience of the theatre or of imaginative writing. What is more, it was written in a hurry, under extreme pressure and mental stress, with the primary purpose of earning Büchner money for his escape from the Grand Duchy of Hessen, where he was in danger of being arrested and imprisoned – probably for the rest of his life – as the co-author of an anonymous revolutionary pamphlet. The other author of the pamphlet, a Lutheran clergyman, killed himself in prison a few days after Büchner's early death. Though the play was published in 1835, after being bowdlerized by Karl Gutzkow, the leader of the Young Germany movement, it was not performed until 1902, sixty-five years after Büchner's death. Karl Gutzkow, who made its publication possible, must have sensed that the play's 'indecencies' were only a superficial aspect of its radical originality; he called Büchner a 'clandestine genius', and though 'genius' is not a word that Büchner himself would have used, no other description fits his case.

Danton's Death was written only three years after Goethe's death, a period of disorientation in German literature, when even Heine could not quite liberate himself from outworn Romantic conventions and dramatists like Grillparzer were trying to write grand blank-verse tragedies in the neo-classical mode evolved by Goethe and Schiller after their *Sturm und Drang* phases. Writers connected with the Young Germany movement wanted a literature that would break with both Romantic and Neo-Classical precedents, but they wrote no plays that have survived either as theatre or as literature. Only Büchner, who died at the age of twenty-three and devoted most of his energy to scientific work, becoming a lecturer in comparative anatomy shortly before his death, succeeded in writing plays that have grown in relevance from decade to decade and established themselves internationally as part of the living theatre.

Even Büchner's radical originality drew on a tradition, but the tradition he drew on had become a 'clandestine' one. In German literature it was the *Sturm und Drang* of the seventeen-seventies and eighties, when plays were written in prose heightened by metaphor and word-play; and the progenitor of these German plays in turn was Shakespeare. Büchner acknowledged his debt both to one of the German *Sturm und Drang* dramatists, Lenz, about whom he wrote a magnificent story, and to Shakespeare.

Büchner regarded himself as a realist, and it was in Shakespeare and the German *Sturm und Drang* dramatists, including the young Goethe, that he found a precedent for his particular kind of realism, a realism psychological and philosophical as well as social. Realism was his justification for the language so offensive to nineteenth-century prudery, and the same kind of language occurs in Shakespeare. On a deeper plane Büchner was obsessed by the realities that confront human beings when they are stripped of all pretence and self-deception, when they come to grips with 'the thing itself' not in the idealistic Kantian sense – Büchner hated philosophical idealism – but in King Lear's when he speaks of 'unaccommodated man' as a 'poor, bare, forked animal'. This existential obsession with rock bottom realities goes some way towards explaining why Büchner, who as an active revolutionary had been too radical for the existing reformist groups, if only by insisting that the true revolutionary factors were economic rather than constitutional, made Danton the hero of his play and Danton at the moment of his utmost disillusionment, face to face with death.

But the word 'hero' could be misleading, since Robespierre too has his moment in the play, and the distinction of Büchner's realism is that it reached out beyond all the accepted notions of heroism and morality to something more fundamental and universal, the human condition itself. Büchner has been called pessimistic and nihilistic. Yet his commitment to 'unaccommodated man' – which made him choose a hero even less heroic than Danton, the half-crazy, half-articulate soldier Woyzeck for a later play – had the intensity of a religious faith. Since it was a commitment not to a faction, ideology or code, but to the 'poor, bare, forked animal' to which any human being can be reduced in extreme circumstances, it served Büchner well as a dramatist. Far from falling into the tendentious didacticism and partisanship of other Young Germany writers, Büchner could create characters from the inside, by self-identification with their conflicting needs and impulses. His social realism demanded a high degree of faithfulness to the documentary sources of all his imaginative works, except the pseudo-Romantic comedy *Leonce and Lena*, but only as far as externals were concerned. Psychological realism demanded something which the documents did not provide – a penetration into human motives which Büchner owed to the complexities of his own nature, to his compassion and empathy and perhaps to his philosophical and scientific preoccupations. *Danton's Death* includes almost literal transcriptions from speeches made by functionaries of the French Revolution, but it also includes variants of passages in Büchner's own letters – not to mention situations for which there is no historical evidence. In other words, Büchner's social realism did not cramp his imagination. He could be true to the social realities of his setting – often with a rigour that anticipated Naturalism – without any loss of linguistic invention or dramatic tension.

If a single word can sum up the distinction of Büchner's art, that word is intensity. There is not a boring or merely functional line of dialogue in his plays. Even where he resorted to the plainest idiomatic diction, as in *Woyzeck*, Büchner attained poetic intensity by his concentration on essentials, on the gesture behind the words. He had an instinctive mastery of speech rhythms as the vehicles of thought and emotion. His prose, therefore, is more truly poetic than most of the blank verse produced by his contemporaries. Structurally, too, he practised a related economy and reduction, as his preference for very short scenes indicates. This formal economy corresponds to the thematic one already outlined – to Büchner's dominant and constant attention to the essentials of the human condition at its barest, 'birth, copulation and death', but also hunger and the need for basic security. His concern with human extremity extended to what are called abnormal states of mind, hallucination and paranoia; and he rendered them with the same precision and power with which he rendered the most commonplace anxieties and desires.

Büchner has been seen as the precursor of almost every kind of theatre that has developed since his lifetime – from Naturalism and Expressionism to the 'epic' and documentary play of our time and the 'theatre of the absurd'. Marxists claim him for socialist realism,

Christian or agnostic existentialists for their variety of humanism. That there is some truth in all these claims is a proof of Büchner's central and pivotal position in the history of drama. Yet it is worth remembering that no sort of historical determinism accounts for that position – somewhere between Shakespeare and the twentieth century – especially since the conflict between freedom and determinism was Büchner's own persistent theme, both in *Danton's Death* and in his other works. Büchner remains an anachronism and an anomaly – a 'clandestine genius'.

Returning to Rilke – A Note

LIKE many people of my generation, I read Rilke devoutly in my teens and twenties, and translated a few of his earlier poems at that period. Then came the long process of learning to write out of my own experience, experience so different from Rilke's that often I had no use for his work. When I did read Rilke in later years, it was the poetry of his middle and later periods that interested me – from the *New Poems* to the uncollected poems and fragments that were gradually made available after his death. Returning to Rilke now, I find that there is something in most of the *New Poems* even that I cannot take – a smoothness, a facility, a lack of friction due to Rilke's singular capacity for what looks like empathy, but isn't. It is a ruthlessly narcissistic assimilation of all that is not himself to the flow of his sensibility – and of his verse. Rilke himself became aware of this. Quite a number of the poems and fragments of his critical years – extending from the completion of the *New Poems* to his death – are attempts to understand and overcome the narcissism. But it was scarcely separable from the extraordinary resourcefulness of his art, the skill with which anything could be made to rhyme with anything, the sheer mastery of the most variously intricate forms. Recently I jotted down a few lines that are both a description and a parody of the manner that aroused my misgivings:

> Free-wheeling round and round his circus ring
> of heart-space, feeling, inwardness he glides
> so easily that none would think he prides
> himself on such a ponderable thing
> as virtuosity. No smugness mars
> his rapt assurance now that upside down
> and back to front he rides the handlebars;
> and never falls. And never once collides
> with anyone, not even with the clown
> who guys his act – to crash, mock-clumsily,
> into the bucket neither seems to see.

In his arena there's no faltering
that's unrehearsed . . .

Yet Rilke was always changing, always experimenting. There is
starkness, and even mischievous humour, in some of the very late
poems and fragments that excited me in my latest re-reading. Whatever one's misgivings about a poet who worked with assumptions
radically foreign to one's own, it is always foolish to reject him totally
if he is as rich, as full of surprises and potentialities, as Rilke.

Yeats's *Memoirs*[*]

Apart from its obvious importance to scholars and specialists, not to mention future biographers of Yeats, this excellently edited and annotated volume could well prove more capable than the more stylized *Autobiographies* of overcoming common prejudices against Yeats's poetry, or against the successive anti-selves that predominate in so much of it. Discriminating readers, of course, need no assurance that Yeats was 'human', that he suffered moral conflicts, nervous breakdowns and sexual deprivation; but for a long time now we have been conditioned to poetic personae that set up no ladders in the 'foul rag-and-bone shop of the heart'. Any poetry that does not make itself thoroughly at home there, offering literal purchases of experience to any comer, tends to be suspect.

In the first draft of the autobiography Yeats hardly dramatizes those quarrels with himself out of which he made his poetry; he is as frank about his personal failures and deficiencies as about his need to overcome them, if only by 'compensating' for them in the most various ways. The study of occultism, for instance, provided him with symbols to be used in poetry; and those symbols, unlike the images of the more advanced French Symbolists, served to break the bounds of an individualism with which he never ceased to grapple, most explicitly in 'Ego Dominus Tuus'. Involvement in politics and in 'theatre business' answered similar needs, because as the *Journal* puts it – artists, 'as seen from life', are 'an artifice, an emphasis, an uncompleted arc perhaps. Those whom it is our business to cherish and celebrate are complete arcs.' To understand that remark in relation to Yeats's development as a poet we have only to read his recollections of fellow members of the Rhymers' Club. They were what Yeats might well have remained if he had not thrown every resource of his will and intellect into the struggle to complete the arc.

The difference between the early draft of the autobiography and

* W. B. Yeats, *Memoirs: Autobiography – First Draft; Journal*, transcribed and edited by Denis Donoghue, Macmillan, London, 1972.

the corresponding sections in the final draft is mainly one of presentation. The previously unpublished references to Yeats's love affair with 'Diana Vernon' are too brief and reticent to amount to the revelation they have been made out to be, but that does not diminish their importance as a corrective to the legend; and even Yeats's relations with the other woman whom he loved and 'could not get' – as he puts it with typical bluntness here – are recorded more vividly in the early draft. What emerges most forcefully throughout both parts of these *Memoirs* is Yeats's psychological acumen, not least in regard to his own motives and impulses. He is candid even about the dual morality to which he resorted at times in his endeavours to bridge the gap between the liberal culture of his time and the heroic archetypes in his imaginative keeping. 'Evil', he writes in the *Journal*, 'comes to us men of imagination wearing as its mask all the virtues.'

Parts of the *Journal*, too, were drawn upon by Yeats for his published autobiographical writings, but the entries made available by Professor Donoghue constitute the most intrinsically valuable portion of this book, because so much of the *Journal* has a direct bearing on Yeats's poetry. It is astonishing to find more evidence not only of the genesis of poems in journal entries but of Yeats's ability to draft a poem in prose, gradually turning an insight or observation into what seems to be a cluster of images and symbols, lyrically conceived. Decades before the publication of the magnificent poem 'Meru' Yeats noted in the *Journal*: 'All civilization is held together by a series of suggestions made by an invisible hypnotist, artificially created illusions. The knowledge of reality is always by some means or other a secret knowledge. It is a kind of death' – an almost literal anticipation of the opening of the late poem. The observation is not strikingly poetic, especially since the metaphor of the 'invisible hypnotist' did not enter into the later crystallization. Yet there is a real and organic connection between the thought of 1909 and the poem of the thirties.

Even those entries not immediately relevant to specific poems are well worth reading in their own right, most often for the acute moral and psychological judgements as conspicuous in them as in the autobiography, as when Yeats remarks on George Russell's followers that 'they trust vision to do the work of intellect' – a criticism that has been applied to Yeats himself in regard to politics – or that 'when these men take to any kind of action it is to some kind of extreme politics.' In the same context he speaks of 'the discipline which enables the most ardent natures to accept obtainable things', and once again it is clear that Yeats is quarrelling with himself as much as with those men. In an earlier entry, already familiar to readers of the published autobiographies, he had written: 'All empty souls tend to extreme opinions. It is only in those who have built up a rich world of memories and habits of thought that extreme opinions affront the sense of probability.' Another of Yeats's insights is of special relevance today, and could be printed on a poster for distribution in many parts of Europe and America: 'Western minds who follow the Eastern way become weak and vapoury because they become unfit for the work forced upon them by Western life.'

Ultimately, though, we are always brought back to Yeats's own preoccupations and antinomies, the tensions from which his poetry sprang. 'All our follies are for the drowsiness of the will', he writes, but also: 'There is no wisdom without indolence.' It is indolence of which Yeats accuses himself elsewhere, in the draft of the autobiography; and the wisdom, too, including simple canniness and common sense, is invigoratingly present in this book.

The Unity of T. S. Eliot's Poetry

No one, I am sure, would now dispute that T. S. Eliot's poetry possesses one kind of unity to a most remarkable degree – a stylistic unity of diction, cadence and imagery. But in any discussion of his work one is likely to hear someone say that he likes the early poems and dislikes the later ones, or that he likes the later ones and dislikes the early ones. The dividing line, it then transpires, is roughly that fixed by Eliot himself when he issued his poems in two small volumes: his early poetry is taken to end with the publication of 'The Hollow Men' in 1925 and includes *The Waste Land*, published three years earlier. His later period begins with the Ariel poems, the first of which appeared in 1927, and includes 'Ash Wednesday' and the *Four Quartets*. It is well known that the dividing line corresponds to a crucial turning-point in Eliot's life, his entry into the Anglican Church. I certainly do not wish to deny the importance of what has been called Eliot's conversion, but I believe that the knowledge of this event has led to an over-emphasis of the difference between his early and later poetry.

Here I am not thinking only, or even primarily, of critics who have expressed an overt bias towards or against Eliot's religious orthodoxy; for very few of us – whether as private readers or as professional critics – are both perceptive and honest enough to make a clear distinction between our judgement of poetry as art and our judgement of poetry as an expression of ideas, attitudes and beliefs. It may be helpful, at this point, to quote from a criticism which does honestly state a bias against Eliot's religious orthodoxy. It is part of George Orwell's review of three of the *Four Quartets*, which he published in 1942: 'If one wants to deal in antitheses', Orwell wrote, 'one might say that the later poems express a melancholy faith, and the earlier ones a glowing despair. They were based on the dilemma of modern man, who despairs of life and does not want to be dead, and on top of this they expressed the horror of an over-civilized intellectual confronted with the ugliness and the spiritual emptiness of the machine age.' The later poems, on the other hand, Orwell accuses of expressing a negative attitude 'which turns its eyes to the past, accepts defeat, writes off earthly happiness as impossible, mumbles about prayer and repentance . . .' Orwell explains his own preference for the early poems by this 'deterioration in Mr Eliot's subject matter'.

The advantage of such a criticism is that we need not accept it if we do not share the clearly formulated prejudices on which it is based. Orwell, it is true, also questions the artistic merit of Eliot's later poetry, but his reasons are so obviously personal that they do not amount to a serious indictment. All that we really learn from his criticism is that he, Orwell, prefers a 'glowing despair' to a 'melancholy faith'.

But those who, like myself, became acquainted with Eliot's later poetry either before reading the early poetry, or at about the same time, are not at all sure that Orwell's antithesis is a valid one. To speak for myself only, I found that the faith expressed in the *Four Quartets* is not always melancholy, and that much of the despair expressed in *The Waste Land* and 'The Hollow Men' is far from glowing; also that all the despair of the early poems is contained in the faith of the later ones, and that much of this faith was already implicit in the early poems, because of the peculiar quality of the despair which they express.

One of Orwell's objections is that in the later poems Eliot 'writes off earthly happiness as impossible'. If by 'earthly happiness' Orwell means a happiness attainable by purely earthly means – as other parts of his review would suggest – his observation is quite correct; but in this respect there is no difference between the early poems and the late. In the early poems, from 'The Love Song of J. Alfred Prufrock' onwards, Eliot inquires into the lives of those who do believe that 'earthly happiness is possible' – 'earthly happiness' in the sense in which I have defined it – and shows that their lives are empty and meaningless:

> For I have known them all already, known them all.
> Have known the evenings, mornings, afternoons,
> I have measured out my life with coffee spoons,
> I know the voices dying with a dying fall
> Beneath the music from a farther room.
>   So how should I presume?

Orwell could accept this kind of comment on life because it is non-committal and oblique; and because it could be interpreted as a comment only on a particular way of life, that of a certain class or social milieu. Such a comment would not conflict with Orwell's own belief that 'earthly happiness' could be brought about by changes in the material world, by social or economic reform. This, however, is a misinterpretation of Eliot's comment: the rest of the poem makes it quite clear that he is not merely satirizing one class or milieu, but every way of life that is based on the pursuit of 'earthly happiness'. Even the love between men and women is included in Eliot's questioning of the values by which the worldly live:

> And I have known the arms already. Known them all –
> Arms that are braceleted and white and bare
> (But in the lamplight, downed with light brown hair!)
> Is it perfume from a dress
> That makes me so digress?
> Arms that lie along a table, or wrap about a shawl . . .

'The Love Song of Alfred J. Prufrock' is a very strange love song indeed; and one would need to be very biased or very perverse to call its ironic scepticism positive, and the answer to it – as provided by the later poems – negative.

It will not be possible here to trace Eliot's attitude to 'earthly happiness' through all his early poems and to show how every question asked in these early poems is answered in the later ones; a few examples will have to suffice. What I hope to show is that these questions, by their very nature, point to the kind of answer given in the later poems; not to a vindication of an 'earthly happiness' that can be attained through the fulfilment of worldly ambitions and desires.

Of the four satirical pieces with an obviously American setting, 'The Boston Evening Transcript', 'Aunt Helen', 'Cousin Nancy' and 'Mr. Apollinax', it could once again be said that they question only a particular way of life, that of a wealthy, educated and leisured class in a certain place at a certain time; but their irony and their weariness go deeper than that. The ironic reference to 'Matthew and Waldo, guardians of the faith, the army of unalterable law' (in 'Cousin Nancy') is no mere accident; for Matthew Arnold and Ralph Waldo Emerson represent an eclectic humanism which is the prevalent substitute for religious faith. Eliot therefore makes a clear connection between the hollow lives led by all the characters in these poems and a philosophical outlook which is by no means confined to themselves.

In 'Mr. Apollinax' Eliot introduces that method of contrast by allusion to myth and literature which he was to use with such powerful effect in *The Waste Land*; no comment on modern society could be more damning than the conclusion, with its return to the tea party with which the poem begins:

> 'He is a charming man' – 'But after all what did he mean?' –
> 'His pointed ears . . . He must be unbalanced,' –
> There was something he said that I might have challenged,
> Of dowager Mrs. Phlaccus, and Professor and Mrs. Cheetah
> I remember a slice of lemon and a bitten macaroon.

A similar impression of lives completely meaningless is left by another poem from Eliot's first collection, 'Rhapsody on a Windy Night'. This poem, too, is set in America, but the scene could be any large city in any western country. After a walk through this city in the early hours of the morning the person of the poem returns to his own lodgings:

> The lamp said
> Four o'clock
> Here is the number on the door.
> Memory!
> You have the key,
> The little lamp spreads a ring on the stairs,
> Mount.
> The bed is open; the tooth-brush hangs on the wall.
> Put your shoes at the door, sleep, prepare for life.
> The last twist of the knife.

In this poem all the imagery is sufficiently general, even universal, to preclude any suggestion that the poet has intended nothing more than a piece of social satire; the preparation for life – which is 'the last twist of the knife' – is the preparation for any life not sustained by a purpose which transcends that life; and the cruel finality of the last image conveys a despair so great that no material remedy could possibly prove effective.

Not all these early poems are cruel. 'Portrait of a Lady' ruthlessly exposes a life based on illusion, but it is also a poem full of pity – the same pity that Eliot expresses at the end of 'Preludes', before juxtaposing another image of cruel indifference.

> I am moved by fancies that are curled
> Around these images, and cling:

> The notion of some infinitely gentle
> Infinitely suffering thing.
> Wipe your hand across your mouth, and laugh;
> The worlds revolve like ancient women
> Gathering fuel in vacant lots.

The pathos of 'Portrait of a Lady' derives from the poet's most delicate treatment of a theme that had rarely been touched upon in poetry at all: this theme is the impossibility of communication, and of communion, between those whose lives are circumscribed by material ends. Eliot conveys this terrible incompatibility between the elderly lady and her young visitor by a characteristic juxtaposition of the tragic with the trivial:

> 'Ah my friend, you do not know, you do not know
> What life is, you should hold it in your hands;
> (Slowly twisting the lilac stalks)
> You let it flow from you, you let it flow
> And youth is cruel, and has no remorse
> And smiles at situations which it cannot see.'
> I smile of course
> And go on drinking tea.

That Eliot's own solution would be a religious one, and that it would take the form of renunciation, is already intimated in the last poem from his first collection, 'La Figlia che Piange'. We are not told who the girl in this poem is; we are told nothing about her and it has even been suggested that she is only the statue of a girl. But there can be no doubt that she symbolizes a leave-taking, a renunciation, which recurs throughout Eliot's later work – often in the form of images closely related to the girl of this early poem:

> Stand on the highest pavement of the stair –
> Lean on a garden urn –
> Weave, weave the sunlight in your hair –
> Clasp your flowers to you with a pained surprise –
> Fling them to the ground and turn
> With a fugitive resentment in your eyes:
> But weave, weave the sunlight in your hair.
>
> So I would have had him leave,
> So I would have had her stand and grieve,
> So he would have left
> As the soul leaves the body torn and bruised.

> As the mind deserts the body it has used
> I should find
> Some way incomparably light and deft
> Some way we both should understand
> Simple and faithless as a smile and shake of the hand . . .

'La Figlia che Piange', too, is a poem of incompatibility, but of an incompatibility affirmed and transcended by renunciation. Much later, in 'Burnt Norton', Eliot identifies his recurrent image of the flower garden, in this case of the 'rose-garden', with 'our first world', that is to say with the garden of Eden. In 'Ash Wednesday', too, he writes of 'the garden where all loves end', meaning the Fall of Man and the origin of that sin which henceforth will attach to every human love. No such connection is made in 'La Figlia che Piange', but we can pursue the development of the garden, the girl and the flower images from this early poem to *The Waste Land*, 'Ash Wednesday', *The Family Reunion* and the *Four Quartets*. In this way the poem assumes a crucial significance and acts as a link between the early and later work.

'Gerontion', which opens Eliot's second collection, published in 1920, foreshadows both the mood and the message of the poetry which he wrote after his entry into the Church of England. Not only does it contain a quotation from an Anglican divine, Launcelot Andrewes, but it contrasts the 'thoughts of a dry brain in a dry season' of an unregenerate old man with 'the juvescence of the year' in which 'Came Christ the tiger'. 'Gerontion', too, is a poem of renunciation, renunciation of worldly ambitions and vanity:

> After such knowledge, what forgiveness? Think now
> History has many cunning passages, contrived corridors
> And issues, deceives with whispering ambitions
> Guides us by vanities . . .

And, as in 'La Figlia che Piange', there is the renunciation of love:

> . . . I that was near your heart was removed therefrom
> To lose beauty in terror, terror in inquisition.
> I have lost my passion: why should I need to keep it
> Since what is kept must be adulterated?
> I have lost my sight, smell, hearing, taste and touch:
> How should I use it for your closer contact.

The satirical pieces in the same collection continue Eliot's inquiry

into the lives of the worldly. As in 'Mr. Apollinax', but with greater
subtlety, he uses the technique of satire by contrast, by the juxtaposition of sordid contemporary scenes with allusions to the myth
and literature of past ages; thus in 'Burbank with a Baedeker:
Bleistein with a Cigar', a study of American tourists in Venice:

> Burbank crossed a little bridge
> Descending at a small hotel:
> Princess Volupine arrived,
> They were together, and he fell.
>
> Defunctive music under sea
> Passed seaward with the passing bell
> Slowly: the God Hercules
> Had left him, that had loved him well.

In the same way the London districts Kentish Town and Golders
Green are contrasted with the splendour of past ages in 'A Cooking
Egg': and once again the sordidness and triviality of modern life are
concentrated into an image of unsatisfactory love between the sexes:

> But where is the penny world I bought
> To eat with Pipit behind the screen?
> The red-eyed scavengers are creeping
> From Kentish Town and Golders Green;
> But where are the eagles and the trumpets?

The waiter in Eliot's French poem of the same period, 'Dans le
Restaurant', is identified with Phlebas the Phoenician, a character
who also appears in *The Waste Land*, where he is not 'wholly distinct
from Ferdinand Prince of Naples' from the one-eyed merchant and
from Tiresias. This device of contracting several characters into one
serves to bring out connections between one age, one civilization, one
milieu and another, but, at the same time, to contrast them for the
sake of satire. Another of these French poems, 'Lune de Miel',
contrasts the boredom and petty annoyances of a modern honeymoon
with one of the sights which the couple fail to visit. This is the
basilica of St Apollinaire en Classe, which

> raide et ascétique,
> Vieille usine désaffestée de Dieu, tient encore
> Dans ses pierres écroulantes la forme précise de Byzance.

However cynical this reference to the basilica may seem, its asceticism and durability compare very favourably with the pleasures

expected, but not experienced, by the young married couple of the poem: the implication is indirect but unmistakable.

It would be gross and presumptuous to include *The Waste Land* in a necessarily rapid survey of this kind. I can only touch on a few aspects of it that relate to my remarks on the shorter poems. The symbol of the waste land itself was already present in 'Gerontion', with its 'old man in a dry month . . . waiting for rain'; in the longer, more complex poem, this symbolism is both extended and clarified.

> He who was living is now dead
> We who were living are now dying
> With a little patience
> Here is no water but only rock
> Rock and no water and the sandy road
> The road winding above among the mountains
> Which are mountains of rock without water . . .

In this arid wilderness, inhabited by those who live only by secular values, every action and every aspiration is meaningless. An erotic encounter between a typist and a clerk exemplifies this lack of spiritual content:

> She turns and looks a moment in the glass
> Hardly aware of her departed lover:
> Her brain allows one half-formed thought to pass:
> 'Well now that's done: and I'm glad it's over.'
> When lovely woman stoops to folly and
> Paces about her room again, alone
> She smoothes her hair with automatic hand,
> And puts a record on the gramophone.

In the fifth and last section of the poem, Eliot refers again to this episode as

> 'The awful daring of a moment's surrender
> Which an age of prudence can never retract
> By this, and this only have we existed.'

It is true that the words spoken by the thunder in *The Waste Land*, by the thunder which heralds in rain and promises salvation from the wilderness, are taken not from a Christian text but from the Hindu Upanishads; but even in the Christian *Four Quartets* there are allusions to Hindu mysticism. Eliot, after all, is not a preacher but a poet; as such, he has always made use of whatever image or reference will best convey his own vision. I think I have said enough about the early work to show that this vision is a consistent one: that it is a vision which questions the lives of the worldly – typical people of our time – *sub specie aeternatis*. Even the most despairing poem of all, 'The Hollow Men' of 1925, continues this questioning; and it not only takes up the image of the waste land – 'the dead land' or the 'cactus land' as it is called here – but by its fragmentary quotations from the litany and the Lord's Prayer suggests, even if it does not wholly embrace, the Christian solution. To the 'dead land' it opposes 'death's dream kingdom', thus confirming the paradox of a life beyond death that is more real than our lives on this earth; for in our present lives

> Between the idea
> And the reality
> Between the motion
> And the act
> Falls the Shadow

and

> . . . Our dried voices when
> We whisper together
> Are quite meaningless
> As wind in dry grass
> Or rats' feet over broken glass
> In our dry cellar.

Eliot's profession of Christian orthodoxy at this point was an event of the greatest importance; but, although it deeply affected his work as a critic, his experiments with drama and his attitude to society, its effect on his lyrical poetry has been exaggerated. Eliot himself has told us 'that the progress of an artist is a continual self-sacrifice, and continual extinction of personality . . . The more perfect the artist, the more completely separate in him will be the man who suffers and the mind which creates; the more perfectly will the mind digest and transmute the passions which are its material.' Because Eliot is a consummate artist, he has always given us the 'objective correlative' of his own experiences, not those experiences themselves. With very few exceptions – such as the choruses from *The Rock*, which were written for a specific occasion and are more dramatic than lyrical – his later poetry is not a didactic exposition of Christian dogma. The style of his later poems, like that of the early ones, is highly individual; yet, to quote his own words once more, 'poetry is not a turning loose of emotion, but an escape from emotion; it is not the expression of personality, but an escape from personality. But, of course, only those who have personality and emotions know what it means to want to escape from these things.'

The essay from which I have been quoting, 'Tradition and the Individual Talent', was published in 1920, that is to say before Eliot's 'conversion'; but the view of the poet's function expounded in it is quite contrary to the views that were current at the time. Eliot's emphasis on the impersonal and super-personal nature of art at a time when all the stress was on individualism and personality points to the conclusion that he was a mystic before he was an orthodox Christian; and it is the mysticism of his later poems, not their orthodoxy, that makes them so difficult to understand. Eliot's mysticism, furthermore, is of a kind that is rare in modern poetry. It is not the mysticism of Rilke's *Duineser Elegien*, for that is a mysticism based on the poetic experience itself, on the poet's transformation of the visible world into poetry. Eliot's mysticism is a much more severe one: for it seeks a reality that is not manifested in the visible world at all and has no use for the sensuous experience by which Rilke apprehended the visible world before transforming it. Whereas Rilke's mysticism is aesthetic, Eliot's is ascetic.

This ascetic mysticism, as I have tried to show, preceded Eliot's profession of Christian orthodoxy; it is present in all the early poems, if only in the form of negation, the negation of worldly values, personal ambition and sexual love. The quotation from St John of the Cross which Eliot prefixed to his dramatic fragment of 1932, *Sweeney Agonistes*, sums up the character of his own mysticism: 'Hence the soul cannot be possessed of the divine union until it has divested itself of the love of created beings'. Rilke began with the love of created beings and, pantheistically, glorified the created world. Eliot began by questioning the reality of created beings and sought communion with the Creator not in, but beyond, the created world. Rilke, of course, was not a Christian poet at all; but even Christian poets like Gerard Manley Hopkins have chosen to praise the Creator by praising created things – an approach much more natural to poets than Eliot's asceticism.

The process of withdrawal, renunciation and depersonalization is carried further in the later poems; it is symbolized by the stairs of 'Ash Wednesday'. But the extreme difficulty of this divestment 'of the love of created things', and the temptation to backslide, is also evident from the same poem, and it is the girl and flower images that convey the soul's attachment to 'created beings':

Blown hair is sweet, brown hair over the mouth blown
Lilac and brown hair:
Distraction, music of the flute, stops and steps of the mind over the
    third stair,
Fading, fading; strength beyond hope and despair
Climbing the third stair.

The Four Quartets are dominated by Eliot's mystical experience; so much so that the poet continually questions the ability of words to convey it. 'The poetry', he says in 'East Coker', 'does not matter'; that is to say, the poetry has become less important than the vision which it serves to embody. Yet the *Four Quartets* are not poems of escape from the temporal plane, for they accept and transcend it. The sordid and senseless world of the early poems is contained in them, as in the section of 'Burnt Norton' which recalls

> . . . the strained time-ridden faces
> Distracted from distraction by distraction
> Filled with fancies and empty of meaning
> Tumid apathy with no concentration
> Men and bits of paper, whirled by the cold wind
> That blows before and after time . . .

'Not here, not here the darkness, in this twittering world', the poet exorcizes these images and turns to the 'internal darkness' which is the 'darkness of God', the 'dark night of the soul'. Thus in 'East Coker':

I said to my soul, be still and let the dark come upon you
Which shall be the darkness of God. As in a theatre
The lights are extinguished, for the scene to be changed
With a hollow rumble of wings, with a movement of darkness on darkness
And we knew that the hills and the trees, the distant panorama
And the bold imposing façade are all being rolled away . . .
. . . I said to my soul, be still, and wait without hope
For hope would be hope for the wrong thing; there is yet faith
But the faith and the love and the hope are all in the waiting.
Wait without thought, for you are not ready for thought:
So the darkness shall be the light, and the stillness the dancing.

    At the same time, Eliot's vision has become wider and nature, too, has received a place in his vision; for having progressed so much further in his spiritual ascent, which is also a descent into the dark, the poet need no longer fear the rose-garden and 'the deception of the thrush'. This development explains the matrimonial dance in 'East Coker' and the affirmation of the 'dignified and commodious sacrament' or marriage – the 'necessary conjunction'; and it also explains the tribute to 'the strong brown God', a pantheistic river-god of 'The Dry Salvages', and Eliot's debt in these four poems to the pre-Socratic philosophers of Greece.

The emphasis now is not so much on the conflict and contrast between the timeless world and the temporal world as on their inter-action and interrelation.

> The point of intersection of the timeless
> With time.

The garden and flower images return and, although they symbolize experience in time, they also participate in the timeless world:

> The laughter in the garden, echoed ectasy
> Not lost, but requiring, pointing to the agony
> Of death and birth.

Even human love is affirmed, though as a beginning, not an end in itself:

> Not less of love but expanding
> Of love beyond desire, and so liberation
> From the future as well as the past.

It is the later poems, then – and especially the *Four Quartets* – in which Eliot suggests that 'earthly happiness' is possible, but possible only if we do not overrate its potentialities and scope. Eliot's own vision is still that of the mystic who has suffered the 'desolation of reality'; yet where the early poems harshly rejected the world, with all its aspirations, activities and pleasures, the later poems make a clear distinction between what is fitting for the mystic and the saint and what is fitting for those – the majority – who have no vocation of that kind. It is a distinction made by the Church also; and it could well be argued that Eliot's conversion has not restricted his vision, as Orwell claims, but helped to extend and enlarge it. Eliot's own experience of the world remains constant, or at least consistent, throughout his early and later work; but his real concern with those who do not and cannot share that experience has caused him to write with uncommon detachment, charity and wisdom about the world of time, which he himself learned long ago to transcend.

Nevertheless it is the asceticism of Eliot's vision that makes his poetry unique, an asceticism combined with worldly experience and sophistication as in none of the mystics to whom he is otherwise related. Even Milton, the so-called Puritan, is a sensualist and a pantheist by comparison; and no wonder, since sensualism and pantheism are not merely creeds congenial to poets, but states of mind hardly separable from the poetic process itself. In Eliot's own words, a poet's mind that is well equipped for its work 'is constantly amalgamating disparate experience: the ordinary man's experience is irregular, fragmentary, chaotic. The latter falls in love, or reads Spinoza, and these two experiences have nothing to do with each other, or with the noise of the typewriter or the smell of cooking; in the mind of the poet these experiences are always forming new wholes.' Well, I very much doubt that the ordinary man – whoever he may be – would fail to get Spinoza mixed up with the state of being in love; but Eliot's statement does bring out an important characteristic of the poetic process. What I have called the sensualism of the poet's state of mind is that same receptiveness to the smell of cooking; and its pantheism is its inherent tendency to discover connections everywhere, to posit a basically monistic universe and restore its wholeness by amalgamating 'disparate experiences'. T. S. Eliot differs from most modern poets in his ability to confine this magical function of the imagination to the poetic process itself, never allowing it to assume the status of a creed. He has achieved a rare discipline and a rare discrimination. Hence his opposition to the Romantics, despite those features of his poetry which strike his younger contemporaries as Romantic (in so far as Symbolism is a development of Romanticism), and his utter dissimilarity from Rilke or Wallace Stevens, whose whole 'philosophy' and religion are analogues of the poetic process. There will always be readers and writers of poetry who prefer that 'life-enhancement', that vindication and celebration of the earthly which the poetic imagination is so well and naturally equipped to provide; but Eliot's way, with its poignant ironies and renunciations, is the more difficult and the more extraordinary.

Edwin Muir

What could that greatness be? It was not fame.
Yet now they seemed to grow as they grew less,
And where they lay were more than where they had stood.
They did not go to any beatitude.
They were stripped clean of feature, presence, name,
When that strange glory broke from namelessness.

Edwin Muir: 'The Heroes'

I

FOR those who responded to him as a man or as a poet, Edwin Muir
had something of the nameless glory, the quiet greatness of these
heroes. Very little personal contact was needed to be aware of him
constantly as a rare individual bound by the 'straitness of sub-
mission', as a dedicated mind. It may be partly because my sense of
indebtedness to Muir has not been diminished by his death that I
feel little inclination to submit his work to any systematic critical
procedure, or attempt to 'place' it in relation to this or that contemporary's. I don't mean by this that I intend to write an extended, and
eulogistic, obituary; by the time I got to know his work – later than
that of many younger poets more widely read in the forties – I had
passed the age of literary hero-worship. Yet I doubt, in any case,
whether a strictly analytical approach would do justice to Muir's
poetry. About his distinction there can be disagreement, but no
argument; it is a totality which some will recognize at once, others
will continue to miss and to deny. Fame, as the poem says, has nothing to do with it; the relative neglect of his work during the greater
part of his life did not harm it, or him, and no amount of posthumous
attention will convince those who find his poetry deficient in
sensuous appeal, excitement and passion. Merely to separate the
'technique' of his verse from his vision would be to offend against
the integrity of his art. 'The word technique', he wrote in a letter,
'always gives me a slightly bewildered feeling; if I can translate it as

skill I am more at home with it, for skill is always a quality of the thing that is being said or done, not a general thing at all. A thing asks to be said, and the only test is whether it is said well.' Muir's own criticism, as well as his poetry, is directed towards the same totality of means and ends.

Edwin Muir's heroism was not of the swashbuckling, his diction not of the word-rattling, kind. As a poet, as a critic and as a man he was equally unassuming; and his utter lack of pretensions was due to a wholeness, an integrity – to repeat a much abused word – that has become so rare as to be incomprehensible to many. At a time when every activity was tending to become a technique, a discipline, an autotelic function not to be related to any other, he persisted in relating everything to everything, and subordinating every activity to one dominant concern. If Edwin Muir was incorruptible – and he has been described as saintlike – it was not because he shrank from corruption, but because he was whole; because his moral vision and his imaginative vision were not in conflict, and both were integral parts of his nature.

Yet he achieved and maintained this integrity in the teeth of circumstances that could hardly have been more adverse. His late development as a poet is often mentioned; but what is much more remarkable is that he became a poet at all, and the kind of poet he was. His *First Poems* were published in 1925, only two years before his fortieth birthday; and only nine of the twenty-four poems that made up this volume appear in the *Collected Poems* prepared by him shortly before his death, several of them with drastic cuts and re-visions. Other poets of this century, such as Wallace Stevens, also emerged late; but for very different reasons. Attentive readers of Muir's *Autobiography* will need no further explanation of his late development or of the blemishes that made him reject more than half of the first, and the whole of his next book of verse, the sequence *Chorus of the Newly Dead* (1926); but a few observations are called for. Edwin Muir was never a young poet, with all the dubious glamour and frequent absurdity that this epithet implies. The young poet, of course, is an overrated phenomenon; but though it is easier to be a young poet than a middle-aged one, and to be an old poet is the greatest achievement of all, there is a very good reason why lyrical poetry should have come to be associated with youth. Lyrical poetry springs most naturally from a state of potentiality, of promise or 'pre-existence', as Hofmannsthal called it; the poetry of experience, of full involvement in life, is both harder to write and less immediately appealing. Much of the lyrical poetry written by older men is the product of a more or less deliberately arrested development; but the true poets of maturity are at once innocent and experienced, so that age itself becomes an irrelevance. From his first collection onwards, Edwin Muir's poetry had this balance between youth and age, innocence and experience. There are retrospective poems in this first collection, and poems of youth regained in his last. This meant that the impact of immediate experience was not, and could not be, Muir's primal concern; nor, for different reasons, could it be the arrangement of sounds and images 'in their own right'.

Edwin Muir received very little schooling, and did not pass through any of those institutions in which poetry is accepted, if not encouraged, as a civilized accomplishment. As Muir himself pointed out in an early 'Note on the Scottish Ballads',* 'it is worth noting that the one or two great poets whom Scotland has produced have been in the ordinary sense uncultivated'. Despite his wide interests and reading in later years, this is true of Muir's beginning. In the *Autobiography* he recalls his first attempts to attain the skill appropriate to the thing: 'Though my imagination had begun to work, I had no technique by which I could give expression to it . . . I wrote in baffling ignorance, blundering and perpetually making mistakes'. He also quotes his friend John Holms's description of him at an earlier period, when his interests were more philosophical than imaginative: 'E. M. is explained by his nationality just as much as by his life. I am sure Muir has never experienced profound emotion through beauty; he has read very little poetry. [His] habit of mind is moral and metaphysical. Any writer not concerned with the universal, or with moral problems from a metaphysical point of view, he is inclined to wash out.' Holms attributes this peculiarity of Muir's to his inherited puritan temper, to his religious experience at the age of fourteen, when he was 'saved' by revivalist preachers, as well as to the national character of the Scots; but he could not know that Muir had experienced very profound emotion through beauty in his early childhood. Muir himself had forgotten it at this time, and it took him most of his adult life to remember. One of his last poems is a 'Complaint of the Dying Peasantry'.

His early youth falls into two distinct phases – distinct is a

* In *Latitudes*, 1924.

euphemism here – his childhood in Orkney and his family's removal
to Glasgow, followed by their decline from the dignity of an ancient
farming community to near-proletarian squalor, then by the death
in rapid succession of his parents and two of his brothers. 'I was too
young for so much death', was Muir's comment in the *Autobiography*;
and he went on to relate how he grew 'silent, absent, dingy and composed' in consequence. The disparity between the two phases led
not to integration, but to self-division, self-estrangement and
traumatic fears. Though he did some writing in his Glasgow years,
and contributed verse and prose to Orage's *New Age* in his middle
twenties, his true literary career did not begin till after his marriage
to Willa Anderson in 1919, and could not begin till after a period of
psychological treatment.*

The wretchedness of these early years is indicated here only
because Muir is often thought of as a poet rather remote from the
social and political issues of his time. This could not be further from
the truth. He came to literature as an outsider when social snobbery
was still hale, hearty and bluff, and outsiders were in no immediate
danger of being hugged to death, like young poets; and he suffered
hardships, losses and degradations that make the complaints of our
present angry young men sound like the yapping of lap dogs. He
became a socialist before socialism was fashionable, or even respectable; and he confronted the realities of Scottish living conditions in
his novel *Poor Tom* (1932), largely based on his own family's experiences in Glasgow, and in *Scottish Journey* (1935), a documentary
study comparable to Orwell's *The Road to Wigan Pier*, published
two years later than Muir's book. His first collection of poems contains ballads written in Scots, and the Scottish literary tradition
never lost its claim on him. True to the injunction in his poem 'The
Journey Back',

> Seek the beginnings, learn from whence you came
> And know the various earth of which you are made,

he devoted his last years to a study of the ballads, left unfinished at
his death. Yet as a poet he could no more identify himself with
Scottish nationalism than with the English political movement of the

---

* The 'brilliant and charming analyst' not named in the *Autobiography* was
Maurice Nicoll, whose later thought and writings might well seem to have some
bearing on Muir's; but Muir was not aware of them when I mentioned Nicoll
to him.

thirties, though he had more personal cause to protest than any of the writers associated with either group.

Muir did not need Yeats to tell him that poetry is not made out of our quarrel with others, but out of our quarrel with ourselves; that it is only through our quarrel with ourselves that we can come to deal truthfully and charitably with the human condition. The unpretentiousness of Muir's poetry and his humility as a man derive from the same recognition. His humility was neither an attitude nor a virtue in any conventional sense, but simply an aspect of his self-knowledge or – this comes to the same thing – of his humanity. From his first book of poems to the last, previously uncollected pieces, he explored a single theme, the relation of the individual life to the whole of life, past, present and future. As he put it in the *Autobiography*, 'Our minds are possessed of three mysteries: where we came from, where we are going and, since we are not alone, but members of a countless family, how we should live with one another.' The political and social problem is included in this preoccupation; specific events and conditions, such as the last war, the impoverishment of Scotland, the plight of refugees, the Communist *coup* in Czechoslovakia, are dealt with more or less overtly in some of the poems, but the particular is always subordinated to the general, the fact to the truth. Despite their rare constancy and unity, neither Muir's preoccupation nor his art was in any way static; in reading the *Collected Poems* one is struck more forcefully than ever by the development and progression of both.

As one would expect after the circumstances of his youth, Muir's first works are pervaded by a sense of duality. His utter estrangement from the false self imposed on him by society – from the clerk in the bone factory – induced a trance-like state in which he could project himself at will into dreams and visions of extraordinary vividness. These dreams and visions provided a store of archetypal images and actions on which he drew all his life; but the more urgent task was to reconcile dream with reality, the dreaming self with the waking self.

Tragic conflict and incompatibility are the theme of his short novel *The Marionette* (1927), an account of the relationship between an idiot child and his father, set in Austria (where Muir became interested in the educational theories of A. S. Neill). Contact between the father's world of adult realities and the son's world of infantile fantasy can only be made by series of delicate experiments, partly unsuccessful, involving dolls and puppets; yet, though father and son come to grow alike in appearance, each remains confined to his own world. This minute and claustrophobic narrative points to Muir's later affinities with Kafka, but it could only have been written while Muir himself suffered from a maladjustment less extreme than the boy's, but also basically due to a conflict between imagination and reality.

Some twenty years later, in his book *The Voyage*, Muir could look back with a certain detachment and irony at the two phases of his youth;

> My childhood all a myth
> Enacted on a distant isle;
> Time with his hourglass and his scythe
> Stood dreaming on the dial . . .
>
> My youth a tragi-comedy,
> Ridiculous war of dreams and shames
> Waged for a Pyrrhic victory
> Of reveries and names,
> Which in slow-motion rout were hurled
> Before sure-footed flesh and blood
> That of its hunger built a world,
> Advancing rood by rood.

'The Myth'

But it is in this collection – in its last pages, to be precise – that Muir began to resolve the dualism of time and eternity, myth and reality, idea and phenomenon, fable and story, which he had perpetually varied and developed in the earlier works. He was approaching his sixtieth year before he was wholly rid of the fear that there might be 'no crack or chink, no escape from Time', as he had written in 'Variations on a Time Theme' (1934).

II

Here it is as well to turn for a moment to Muir's critical works of the early period. Socialism and Social Credit were two of the movements that helped Muir to cope with the economic realities of the age; but 'how we should live with one another' was not his only problem. His personal deprivation was too radical, and his personal liberation not only from social squalor, but from the Calvinist narrowness of his surroundings, demanded measures at once more drastic and more appropriate to his own case. Intellectual and aesthetic emancipation were the greater need. For a time he came under the influence of Heine, then of Nietzsche. Of the two, Nietzsche's influence was far more than a youthful intoxication, the leaven in Muir's first literary works; its importance is such that it needs separate treatment.

Anyone who comes to Muir's brilliant critical books *We Moderns** and *Latitudes* from his later works cannot fail to be amazed by the entirely different personality that meets him in these books. The Muir of these early essays, epigrams and aphorisms is an *esprit fort*, a sophisticated, cynical, utterly individualistic transvaluator of all values – in short, a Nietzschean. It is the second, but chronologically earlier, section of *Latitudes* that propounds the doctrine of life and love as play, of 'absolute mastery over oneself and the world', of 'life instead of Utopia', and tells us that 'the creative thinker does not need salvation; he brings it'. Whatever else it may be – and it shows extraordinary psychological penetration – this book is not humble. Some of the aphorisms remain valid. 'The unfulfilled desires of the virtuous are evil', with its corollary, 'the unfulfilled desires of the evil are good;' and 'The intensity of the unconscious is poetry; the intensity of the conscious is wit.' Or, more profound than these, and more characteristic of Muir; 'There is a mystery of stupidity as well as mystery of genius. The philosopher is an enigma to the average man, but not a greater one than the average man is to the philosopher.' Yet, in its insistence on the antinomy between genius and the average man, the book is far removed from the poet who was to write: 'It is easy for the false imagination to hate a whole class; it is hard for the true imagination to hate a single human being.'

In the *Autobiography* Muir tells how this Nietzschean arrogance conflicted with his socialism; how he came to see Nietzsche's choice as a 'self-crucifixion out of pride, not out of love', and soon rid himself of all his Nietzschean affectations of super-manhood, partly through his psychological analysis. What is not so well known is how much of Nietzsche's doctrine Muir retained to the end. In his fine poem 'The Recurrence' (from *The Narrow Place*, 1941), the person of Nietzsche, the self-proclaimed Anti-Christ, fades beside the reality of Christ; but the title itself points to what it was in Nietzsche's doctrine that continued its hold over Muir's imagination.

* Published in 1918 under the pseudonym Edward Moore.

> Nothing was ever done
> Till it was done again
> And no man was ever one
> Except through dead men.

'Twice-Done, Once-Done' (from *The Voyage*, 1946)

The idea of the 'eternal recurrence' remained essential to Muir's vision, however modified by Platonic and Christian elements. Nietzsche's cosmology, Plato's metaphysics and Christ's ethic of love are at first opposed, then blended, and finally fused in Muir's poetry.

It is equally true that Muir's total identification with Nietzsche's attitude proved as unprofitable to his criticism as to his poetry, because it was a barrier against the humanity that became the basis of both. But part of his second critical book, and the whole of the next, *Transition* (1926), confront Scottish, foreign and contemporary English literature from a point of view quite independent from Nietzsche. The essays on the ballads, Burns and George Douglas in the second collection, those on Joyce, Lawrence, Virginia Woolf, Aldous Huxley, T. S. Eliot and Edith Sitwell in the third, and the essay on Arnold Bennett contributed to Edgell Rickword's *Scrutinies* (1928), are authentic stages both in Muir's development as a critic and in his progress towards self-knowledge. 'Reality can be attained just as surely through criticism as through any other form of literature,' he wrote in *A Plea for Psychology in Literary Criticism*, and his own essays are the proof.

In these early critical works, from *We Moderns* to *The Structure of the Novel*, Muir came to grips with 'the problems of our time, which are so defacing, so unlike, in their search for unsightly things, the problems of more human eras' ('A Note on Ibsen'); doing so he eliminated what was false in his own aims, and defined his own humanity. In exactly the same way, Muir's residence in Italy, Austria, Germany and Czechoslovakia at the same period served to make him aware of his own roots; the exploration of foreign countries – *Latitudes* contains an essay on Prague – and the exploration of various literatures were what Hölderlin called 'colonization', a process which necessarily precedes the most difficult task of all, that of 'going to the source' and 'learning what is proper to oneself'. Thus, when Muir remarks that 'in no poetry, probably, in the world is there less imagery than in the ballads,' and that this is due to a 'terrific simplicity', he is also pointing to a characteristic of his own, still unwritten poetry; and he attributes the same starkness to 'that something materialistic in the imagination of the Scots, which is one of their great qualities'. The admirable essay 'North and South' is another instance of Muir's search for his own place within the European tradition, as well as the record of a discovery that is part of his permanent debt to Nietzsche: 'that Western Europe is, like Egypt and Greece, eternal whether it passes away or remains; and the rise and fall of civilizations are not to be mourned with irrevocable sorrow by those who have learned the secret of making them immortal'.

With *Transition* and *The Structure of the Novel* Muir had arrived at criticism proper, less autobiographically revealing than the first two books, because more certain of its own point of view. The later criticism does not concern me here. His last critical book, *Essays on Literature and Society*, appeared in 1949. Perhaps it was an exaggeration to say that the neglect suffered by Muir did his work no harm, for the great majority of readers remember him only for the most ephemeral part of his critical work, his book-reviewing in later years. If it was this neglect that confined him to journalism even in his late maturity, the implications are distressing enough; but it certainly did not embitter Muir or prevent him from writing poetry right up to his last illness and death.

III

The early critical works cleared the way for the first poems. In a certain sense it is true to say that the whole of Muir's poetry was a search for lost time, a bridge thrown over the gulf of his lost youth to his island childhood. But this gulf did not widen with increasing age; the paradox of time in his poetry, very much like that in Proust's novel, is that the gulf can be closed in the end by faithful and constant recapitulation. I have followed the *Autobiography* in stressing the personal origin of Muir's need to regain lost time; but it is a foolish and inhuman prejudice to assume that what is personal in origin must remain so in relevance and effect. A truthful and thoroughgoing subjectivity turns into its opposite. The self of Muir's poetry is so thoroughly stripped of circumstance, pose and vanity, as to be depersonalized; whereas the objectivity of those who cannot face the truth about themselves never penetrates beyond these accretions.

'Only the personal is for ever incontrovertible,' Nietzsche remarked.

Even in the *First Poems* Muir made his own dreams and memories the starting-point of a journey into history and myth. The 'Ballad of Hector in Hades' derives from a childhood fear; the 'rough grey stones spotted with lichen' observed at Wrye in his early childhood occur in more than one of these poems, written some twenty-five years later. But many of these first poems are merely nostalgic in the manner of Heine, instead of juxtaposing past and present experience, as the later poems do, so as to defeat time and lay bare the heraldic emblem. It is beyond my scope here to trace the process from poem to poem, from book to book, or to do more than indicate some of the obstacles. One of them is the experience of men wholly absorbed in 'the common dream', in Yeats's sense, of men in their temporal, material and animal aspects. The *Autobiography* records one instance of this experience, Muir's vision of the animal faces of fellow passengers in a tram. Many of the earlier poems are tragic because they see no release from this state, other than death; as late as *The Voyage* (1946), Muir could be haunted by this anti-vision, as in the poem 'Epitaph':

> Into the grave, into the grave with him.
> Quick, quick, with dust and stones this dead man cover
> Who living was a flickering soul, so dim
> He never was truly loved nor truly a lover.
>
> Since he was half and half, now let him be
> Something entire at last, here in this night
> Which teaches us its absolute honesty
> Who stay between the light and the half-light . . .

This anti-vision is related to the experience of Scotland's impoverishment by Calvinism, Puritanism and material exploitation; significantly, it was in Italy that the breach was healed once and for all, that Muir grasped the mystery of the Incarnation. Few of his poems, even those about the war, are more bitter than 'Scotland 1941':

> . . . But Knox and Melville clapped their preaching palms
> And bundled all the harvesters away,
> Hoodicrow Peden in the blighted corn
> Hacked with his rusty beak the starving haulms.
> Out of that desolation we were born.

Even Burns and Scott become 'sham bards of a sham nation'.

It was not till the Italian transfiguration of all his past experience that Muir emerged finally from the labyrinth of 'the common dream' – though to him community with all men was part of the truth into which he emerged. In the light of Italy, the transfiguring light, both anti-visions are banished once and for all in a poem from his last collection:

> The windless northern surge, the seagull's scream,
> And Calvin's kirk crowning the barren brae.
> I think of Giotto, the Tuscan shepherd's dream,
> Christ, man and creature in their inner day.
> How could our race betray
> The Image, and the Incarnate One unmake
> Who chose this form and fashion for our sake?

'The Incarnate One'

Yet Nietzsche and Plato had their part in this late affirmation. The 'eternal recurrence' prepared Muir for the final merging of time and eternity, phenomenon and idea, the liberation from Plato's cave. And dreams remained the source of some of his purest poems. A late poem, like 'The Combat' (in *The Labyrinth*, 1949), based on an early dream, is one of the closest approximations in poetry to Kafka's world of absolute fiction – so subjective in origin, so inexhaustible and universal in effect; and Edwin and Willa Muir, of course, were Kafka's translators.* In comparison, even myth seems an impure form, too much tied to historical and local associations. That is one reason why some of Muir's poems break the unity of particular myths, relating one to another, or penetrating beyond them into pure imagination.

If there seems to be a contradiction between pure imagination and a lack of striking imagery that has been held against Muir, what is overlooked is that no prominent image or metaphor is needed where the whole poem passes beyond analogy, beyond allegory, to

---

* Not only Muir's admiration for Kafka, but his understanding of the works, deepened with time. The sonnet to Kafka in *One Foot in Eden*, strangely parallelled by Muir's tribute to Milton in the same collection, testifies to the admiration. In his Introductions to the translations, Muir had interpreted Kafka's fiction as allegory; it was not till 1947 that he corrected this view and stressed the purely imaginative character of Kafka's works; this important disclaimer, contributed to a Czech publication, was subsequently published in the volume *Essays on Literature and Society* (1949). Muir's realization that there is no key to Kafka's fiction has a direct bearing on his own later works.

render absolute fictions like 'The Combat'. Kafka's style, too, is uncommonly bare, literal and unfigurative. Where Muir attained such immediacy of conception, there is no need for further explanations, such as his nationality, his inherited Puritanism, his native landscape, dominated by sea and rock, or his Platonism:

> And sometimes through the air descends a dust
> Blown from the scentless deserts of dead time
> That whispers: Do not put your trust
> In the fed flesh, or colour, or sense or shape.
> This that I am you cannot get in rhyme.

'The Journey Back' (from The Labyrinth)

During the last fifteen years or so of his life Muir did succeed in getting it in rhyme, or in the blank verse of his meditative poems (occasionally Wordsworthian when it is retrospective, but more often quite unlike any that has been written in English). I wish I had space to quote at length from poems like 'The Return', 'The Transfiguration', 'The Labyrinth' or 'The Child Dying', the love poems, so much more than passionate, which Muir never ceased to write until his death, lyrics like 'The Late Wasp' and 'The Late Swallow', reflections on his own art, like 'All we who make things transitory and good', 'Soliloquy' and 'The Emblem', or prophetic poems like 'Prometheus' and 'The Horses'. But I shall conclude with a few remarks on the selection of the *Collected Poems* and on the last section, the poems previously uncollected.

IV

Even in a purely material and quantitative sense, Muir succeeded in regaining his lost youth; his late beginning was amply compensated by his capacity to grow and change to the very end. This capacity was such that the last two years of his life, the period following the completion of *One Foot in Eden*, must be regarded as a distinct phase. *The Labyrinth* celebrates Muir's emergence from the maze of temporal phenomena. *One Foot in Eden* is pervaded by the transfiguring love of the 'Song':

> Sunset ends the day,
> The years shift their place,
> Under the sun's sway
> Times from times fall;

> Mind fighting mind
> The secret cords unwind
> No power can replace:
> Love gathers all.

In this collection, Muir appears to come closer than before to Christian doctrine; at least his acceptance of both good and evil, harmony and strife, innocence and corruption, is rendered in symbols largely taken from biblical sources, though Prometheus and Oedipus share in the transfiguring love. I am not competent to discuss the theological implications of Muir's treatment of Eden and the Fall as archetypes of human experience, or to decide how far it would satisfy the requirements of any sectarian orthodoxy. However, since more than one recent writer on Muir has in fact claimed such orthodoxy for him, or claimed him for such orthodoxy, and since this misunderstanding is likely to be perpetuated despite the evidence of the definitive *Collected Poems*, it is necessary to state once more that neither Muir's Italian illumination, nor his earlier awakening to the significance of the Lord's Prayer, was a religious conversion in any accepted sense of the word.

At the period when he was writing the poems in *One Foot in Eden*, Muir himself drew attention to the imaginative aspect of the conciliatory and transfiguring power, akin to divine grace, that dominates the book. 'Perhaps in the imagination of mankind the transfiguration has become a powerful symbol, standing for many things, among them those transformations of reality which the imagination itself creates', he said in 1952.* The word absolute has occurred in my essay; but it was applied to Muir's imagination, not to his beliefs. 'Shortly before he was taken off to hospital,' Mrs Willa Muir has recorded in a letter, 'he said to me, with great urgency: "There are no absolutes, no absolutes." He was then in a confused state, but he said it with such force that it was poignant. I said: "No, darling, there are no absolutes at all," and he was comforted. I don't know myself what to make of it, unless he meant that even death was not an absolute; but there it is.'

Whatever interpretation we give to these words, and whatever weight, the evidence of Muir's selection from the published volumes is conclusive in one respect. The *Collected Poems* volume omits all

* From a broadcast in the Scottish Home Service. Quoted from J. C. Hall's monograph, *Edwin Muir* (Longman's, Green; for the British Council, 1956).

those poems from *One Foot in Eden* which could possibly qualify as Christian devotional or apologist verse: 'The Christmas', 'The Son', 'Lost and Found', and 'The Lord' (a refutation of atheism). The rejection is significant, because only one poem, 'Isaiah', is omitted from *The Narrow Place*, only two relatively slight lyrics from *The Voyage*, no poem at all from *The Labyrinth*; and the rejection of these later poems cannot be attributed to any but the obvious motive. Clearly Muir was anxious to remain uncommitted to the last; a visionary poet, deeply concerned with the example and teaching of Christ, not a Christian poet.

The crucial difference may well lie in Muir's permanent debt to the concept of 'eternal recurrence' (adapted by Nietzsche from the pre-Socratic philosophers), which can lend no absolute significance to history or to any single historical event, requires neither personal immortality nor personal redemption, but only a recognition of the eternal pattern that underlies every individual destiny, and affirms this life for the pattern's sake. Even in the title poem of *One Foot in Eden* the emphasis lies on the state of man after the Fall, transformed by the memory of Eden, not on any future life, redemption or paradise regained:

> What had Eden ever to say
> Of hope and faith and pity and love
> Until was buried all its day
> And memory found its treasure trove?
> Strange blessings never in Paradise
> Fall from these beclouded skies.

The poet who arrived at this affirmation was 'time's true servant' ('The Return'), and what he affirmed was the whole of his past life, errors, perplexities, sufferings and all, even 'the famished field and blackened tree' of the industrialized Scotland where this poem must have been written, though its imagery also points back to the Glasgow of his lost youth. Perhaps it is the personal approach, in the end, that does least violence to the mysteries celebrated by Muir, rather than any attempt to define them in philosophical or theological terms.

Incapable though he was of pose and mystification – few poets have written more honestly about themselves than Muir in the *Autobiography* – it is as a mystery that Muir regarded his own art. Even memory does not account for it in his last word on the subject, his posthumous lines, 'The Poet':

And in bewilderment
My tongue shall tell
What mind had never meant
Nor memory stored.
In such bewilderment
Love's parable
Into the world was sent
To stammer its word.

What I shall never know
I must make known.
Where traveller never went
Is my domain.
Dear disembodiment
Through which is shown
The shapes that come and go
And turn again.

Heaven-sent perplexity –
If thought should thieve
One word of the mystery
All would be wrong.
Most faithful fantasy
That can believe
Its immortality
And make a song.

V

The poems not previously published in book form have been sub-
divided by Mrs Muir and Mr J. C. Hall into those that appeared in
periodicals before Muir's death or were sent by him to his publisher,
those found in typescript after his death but never previously published or submitted, and those found only in manuscript. None of
the poems is dated; but the first section alone bears out T. S. Eliot's
seemingly cryptic statement, 'old men ought to be explorers.'

The opening religious sonnet may be so close to the poems rejected
from *One Foot in Eden* as to make its inclusion a little puzzling; but
it has a directness and informality of tone which the others lack.
And it is counterbalanced by that ironic and subtle poem, written
during Muir's year at Harvard, 'The Church', comparable in its
complexities and reservations to Philip Larkin's 'Church Going';
but Muir's allegiance not to any established rite, but rather to a

Christianity still to be realized, makes it incomparably more positive in its conclusion:

> I look at the church again, and yet again,
> And think of those who house together in Hell,
> Cooped by ingenious theological men
> Expert to track the sour and musty smell
> Of sins they know too well;
> Until grown proud, they crib in rusty bars
> The Love that moves the sun and the other stars.
>
> Yet fortune to the new church, and may its door
> Never be shut, or yawn in empty state
> To daunt the poor in spirit, the always poor.
> Catholic, Orthodox, Protestant, may it wait
> Here for its true estate.
> All's still to do, roof, window and wall are bare.
> I look, and do not doubt that He is there.

The poem 'Salem, Massachusetts' applies the same serious irony and almost satirical realism to the contrast between past witch-hunts and present 'business men from Boston'. As for Muir's concern with the future in these last poems – 'old men ought to be explorers' – it distinguishes them not only from much of his earlier work, with its inevitably personal preoccupation, but from most of the work of his younger contemporaries. The visions of future cataclysms, 'After a Hypothetical War', 'After 1984', 'The Last War' and 'The Day before the Last Day', are only the most obvious examples. Even where the theme is retrospective, as in the strange sequence 'Images', the poem devoted to the transfigured memory of Muir's two brothers, or the soliloquy of his rakish cousin Sutherland in heaven, 'There's nothing here I can take into my hands', Muir's resolution of his own conflicts allows him to explore new possibilities of mood, tone and diction. The poem 'Impersonal Calamity', in fact, shows why a generalized sympathy, an 'objective' or ideological humanitarianism, is powerless; what we have not known and suffered, we can neither comprehend nor relieve;

> Respectable men have witnessed terrible things,
> And rich and poor things extraordinary,
> These murder-haunted years. Even so, even so,
> Respectable men seem still respectable,
> The ordinary no less ordinary.

> For our inherited features cannot show
> More than traditional grief and happiness
> That rise from old and worn and simple springs.
> How can an eye or brow
> Disclose the gutted towns and the millions dead?

'Ballad of Everyman' and 'Nightmare of Peace' grapple with the related problem of men enslaved by the very ideologists who offer them liberation, only to 'flatter and rob the ignorant clown'. Muir's own capacity for sympathy, rooted in experience of hardships overcome, is evident in all these poems; quite especially in 'The Refugees Born for a Land Unknown', with its insight into the deepest alienation of all, the loss of reality:

> . . . And now with alien eyes I see
> The flowering trees on the unreal hills,
> And in an English garden all afternoon
> I watch the bees among the lavender.
> Bees are at home, and think they have their place,
> And I outside.

'Petrol Shortage', like the earlier poem 'The Horses', testifies to the eternal recurrence in history, a pattern similar to that traced by Muir's personal life and vision:

> The cycle will come round again,
> Earth will repair its broken day,
> And pastoral Europe dream again
> Of little wars waged far away.

Plato, too, receives a final explicit tribute – 'The Poet', quoted above, was indirectly one – in what was almost certainly Muir's last poem, and it follows a tribute to his own beginning, a return to the source:

> I have been taught by dreams and fantasies
> Learned from the friendly and the darker phantoms
> And got great knowledge and courtesy from the dead
> Kinsmen and kinswomen, ancestors and friends
> But from two mainly
> Who gave me birth . . .
>
> And now the time grows shorter, I perceive
> That Plato's is the truest poetry,
> And that these shadows
> Are cast by the true.

Edwin Muir's Letters*

'I'm the round peg in a square hole', Edwin Muir wrote to George
Barker in 1936; 'or rather, being an angular Scotsman, the square
peg in a round hole; I've spent half my life rubbing off my corners
instead of sharpening them, like the rest of my countrymen, and I
don't know whether even now I fit the beautiful perfect O of poetry
very comfortably.' The remark seems casual, if not light-hearted;
but Edwin Muir was not given to self-comment, self-analysis or self-
confession, let alone self-dramatization – and that applies to his
letters as to his autobiography and his poems. So the remark is
arresting. The more one considers it, the more extraordinary, the
more apt, and the more disturbing it becomes. What is that 'beautiful
perfect O of poetry' for which Muir had to rub off his corners? The
whole anomaly of his position as a writer – 'alienation' would be the
word if it weren't so inappropriate to a man who made so little fuss
about himself, who blamed no one for hardships and humiliations
that often came close to breaking him – is in those words.

> My life had been a continuous enemy of my inner development. At
> 14 I had had to begin work in a commercial office – hours 9 to 6; at 18 I
> was thrown upon the world to live on the 14/- a week that I earned at
> the cost of ill-health and psychological misery; and I am still a little
> surprised to this hour that all this time I read, learned to love music
> and, being a Scotsman, speculation, without knowing for years a single
> person to whom I could speak of those things. [To Sydney Schiff,
> 1924.]

The story is familiar to readers of Muir's autobiography, and the
letters add only a few details of the early life. Regrettably, the
selection includes no letter written before March 1919, when Muir
was thirty-one, and had already made a false start as a writer with
the Nietzschean *We Moderns*. Yet personal letters are a different
medium. Quite apart from the pleasure of being in this poet's

* *Selected Letters of Edwin Muir*, ed. P. H. Butter, Hogarth Press, London, 1974.

company once more, the book will be valuable to every reader of Muir's poems. It also complements the critical writings, as in the letters to Schiff about Wyndham Lewis, Joyce and Lawrence.

Some of Muir's countrymen found it hard to forgive him for not sharpening his corners. In fact, he wrote some of his early poems in Scots and returned to that practice as late as 1940, though he never turned it into a programme. Again and again he expressed his hope that Scotland would become a 'Socialist republic', but after associations with both Nationalist and Marxist groups, and even before his direct experience of the Communist take-over in Czechoslovakia, he was too discriminating and scrupulous to be a party man. As early as the twenties he was extraordinarily sensitive to the crypto-fascist tendencies in much of the 'advanced' literature of the time, as to the dangers of strange accordances or reversals of left and right, brought home to him by his own interest in Social Credit. A more deep-seated difficulty had to do with his origins. His Scottish roots were in a community which he remembered as being classless and uncompetitive. He wrote to Stephen Spender in 1936:

> I can see that it is right you should care more for public things than for personal things, and that public things should rouse in you an emotion as spontaneous as a personal emotion. I see that, but I can't bring about the necessary transformation in myself, perhaps because I was born in a different age, and on the top of that in a different world; for the Orkney Islands where I passed my childhood was at that time the same as they had been two hundred years before; untouched still by Industrialism, and still bound to an old co-operative life which preceded that: the very idea of competition was unknown. That really means that I was born over two hundred years ago, or perhaps more, so no wonder if my poetry is an acquired taste, and no wonder if I find difficult what is not easy even to your generation.

After 1925, when Muir's first book of poems was published by Virginia and Leonard Woolf, it often looked as though Muir had been admitted to the English establishment; but the awkwardness that was Muir's honesty and loyalty to his roots never permitted any kind of assimilation. Bloomsbury might forgive him, conditionally, for being a peasant, but he would not do Bloomsbury the favour of behaving like one. Besides, for the intellectual emancipation which he later recognized to have been false Muir had turned to Nietzsche, instead of the French writers that would have made him respectable as a convert, and he continued to discover German or Austrian writers outside the Bloomsbury pale. He described the England of 1924 as 'a standing pool'. 'The English critics are a class who, beneath their reading and equipment, have the prejudice of the English man in the street that culture does not matter.' Beneath his own far-ranging intellectual interests Edwin Muir retained a single-minded seriousness and angularity that made him 'dislike felicities from the bottom of my heart'. Of D. H. Lawrence he wrote in a letter of 1924 that 'he is more interested in language than in his subject matter, and his interest in the one gets between us and the other – a very fundamental sin against art, it seems to me.' Nearly thirty years later, in 1953, he wrote to George Mackay Brown that 'so much modern literature has come out of hatred, or disgruntle-ment, or what people call sophistication, which seems to me the most vulgar thing in the world.' That is hardly the conviction of a man who has made his peace with Bloomsbury. As for the 'success' that Muir may also have looked like 'enjoying' after his exceptionally late start as a writer, Professor Butter mentions in a note that only 'some eighty copies' of Muir's novel *Poor Tom* were sold.

That brings me back to the 'beautiful perfect O of poetry' and the peculiar awkwardness that keeps Muir's poetry an 'acquired taste', even now. Like the makers of the popular ballads that were Muir's starting-point in poetry, and the subject of a last critical project cut off by his death, he could not bring himself to treat words as any-thing but the transparent vehicle of 'subject matter'. Any verbalizing for verbalizing's sake, or for the sake of felicities, would have revolted him as a kind of self-indulgence or exhibitionism. Even wit was denied to him for the same reason, after the fierce satirical wit borrowed from Nietzsche for *We Moderns*. Yet neither did his Orcadian origin provide him with linguistic or formal resources capable of grappling with the sort of experience that had begun to be his when his family moved to Glasgow. Hence the acute dis-crepancies between the 'story' and the 'fable' – a constant danger to his person and his work; and hence, in his early poems, the lack of sensuousness and particularity that left so much suspended in verbal thin air, though no one who understands Muir will ever doubt the genuineness of the experience and vision that were his 'subject matter'. Even the later poems don't sweep their readers away with powerful rhythms, obtrusive metaphors or felicities of melopeia. Few of his poems are immediately 'memorable'; but on re-reading them one may have the curious sensation of rediscovery, of having known them without knowing it. In their unassertive way almost all his later poems have a rightness that is rarer and more enduring than the qualities he had to deny them, out of a deep necessity of his nature. A taste for them, even now, is well worth acquiring.

It could also be that the timeless concerns that made Muir anachronistic in his lifetime will become topical and 'relevant' after his death, because the industrial age he could never more than half accept has entered a phase that is dubious, to put it mildly. If the signs of exhaustion are not a false alarm, and not even a nuclear disaster is needed to put an end to the age of greed, his two-hundred year-old awareness may have more to teach us than the political divisions that would be superseded by its demise. Not that his prose works, and a few of his poems, failed to come to grips with the world in which, right up to the end, he had to struggle for a modest living. One thing that makes these letters moving – and one wishes that more of them will be found and published – is the fund of quiet strength in the man that brought his work to a late fruition, though everything was against him – the 'square peg in a round hole'.

Egon Schiele: The Background

EGON SCHIELE'S active life as an artist almost exactly spanned the last decade of the Austrian Empire and of a European order dominated by the upper middle class. Even in Austria, for all its notorious traditionalism in matters of taste, this decade was one of feverish productivity and innovation. Feverish, because the artists and intellectuals worked like those consumptives of whom it is said that a presentiment of their early death compels them to achieve within a few years what healthy men could afford to spread over half a century. Such presentiments do, in fact, abound in the literary works of Schiele's contemporaries, such as the apocalyptic landscapes and townscapes of the Austrian Expressionist poet Georg Trakl (1887–1914) and the Berlin Expressionist poet Georg Heym (1887–1912). In Trakl's poems there is a pervasive sense of decay; in Georg Heym's, and in those of the Alsatian poet Ernst Stadler (1883–1914) there are prophecies of war, revolution and cataclysm that foreshadow the historical events – in terms of the imagination, if not of literal prophecy.

New movements, trends and styles jostled one another with such urgency and impatience that it remains difficult even now to impose any satisfactory order on the *embarras de richesse* of that decade. Spokesmen and theorists of the avant-garde like the poet Guillaume Apollinaire, who was closely in touch with the painters until his early death in 1918, could not help contradicting themselves in their effort to keep up with the work actually being produced. Apollinaire alone coined enough new names for the new styles and movements to provide for the needs of any other decade. There is no need to list them here, especially since many of them seem inapposite, meaningless or positively misleading in retrospect. Even the term Expressionist was applied at one time to every kind of new German art, from the dynamic representationalism of Kokoschka to the abstractions of Kandinsky or Klee. What is important in our context is that art itself was in a state of flux scarcely paralleled in any other period. Cubism, Futurism, Expressionism and Dadaism – to pick out only a few of the principal trends – were so close together in time as to be almost inextricable even in certain individual artists, let alone in groups or movements.

In Austria, and in Germany to a considerable extent, the situation was further complicated by the relatively late arrival of pre-modernist movements like Naturalism and Symbolism. In 1908, for instance, the noise of the battle for Naturalism was still reverberating in the German theatre while Neo-Romantic symbolism was flourishing – even in some of the works of Gerhart Hauptmann, the leading German Naturalist playwright – and Oskar Kokoschka had left both behind in his extraordinary little play *Murder the Hope of Women*, now rightly regarded as the first Expressionist play and performed, in Vienna of all places, in that year. Yet Kokoschka's play shows striking affinities with some of the dramatic works sketched, but neither completed nor published, at about the same period by the Austrian poet and dramatist Hugo von Hofmannsthal, who is usually regarded as a Neo-Romantic with decidedly traditionalist and conservative leanings. Hofmannsthal, however, sympathized with the work and aspirations of the Wiener Werkstätte; and Gustav Klimt, who influenced both Schiele and Kokoschka, was deeply indebted to the English aesthetic movement and decorative art of the eighteen-nineties, and these were of exemplary importance to Hofmannsthal also.

This overlapping of styles and movements was not peculiar to Austria, though Austrian artists do feel a peculiar need to relate themselves both to the immediate and to the more distant past. In one's approach to the work of any important Austrian artist of that decade one must consider this need as well as the revolutionary turmoil of those years. Much as we hear these days about communications, that miraculous decade was internationalist to a degree scarcely comprehensible now. To be a modern artist was to be a citizen of the world, whatever one's political views or allegiances. Not the least of the tragic ironies of that decade is that the revolutions anticipated by its artists were to usher in a new nationalism and a new bigotry. Ernst Stadler, once a Rhodes scholar at Oxford, devoted much of his energy and enthusiasm to the study and translation of English and French literature and to the cause of international understanding, only to be killed on the Western Front instead of going out to Canada, as he had planned to do in that year. That death is as symbolic as the deaths of Charles Sorley, with his interest in German poetry, or of Apollinaire, the early champion of Italian and Russian Futurism, on the other side.

Schiele, too, was forced to look beyond the wide frontiers of Austria. From its first issue in 1910 until 1918, when it became committed to the extreme left, the German avant-garde periodical *Die Aktion* exemplified both the internationalism of the decade and its fluidity. The visual artists whose work was represented in *Die Aktion* in those eight years included Delacroix, Daumier, Cézanne, Toulouse-Lautrec, Derain, Matisse, Picasso, Archipenko, Soffici, Heckel, Schmidt-Rottluff and Hodler, as well as Egon Schiele. Though, together with *Der Sturm*, *Die Aktion* was the principal mouthpiece of German modernism, and of Expressionism in particular, its literary contributors were no less various; they ranged from Flaubert to Strindberg, from Oscar Wilde to Péguy, from G. K. Chesterton to André Gide, from d'Annunzio to Marinetti, from Richard Dehmel and Maximilian Harden – members of the Naturalist generation – to the innovators Robert Musil and Gottfried Benn.

Another outstanding characteristic of that decade was the interpenetration of all the arts. The architect Adolf Loos – who, incidentally, brought back many dynamic ideas from America – exerted as powerful an influence on the writers as on the painters of the Austrian avant-garde. Karl Kraus, another powerful influence, focused his searching and formidable glance on every field of public and cultural life, including the newspapers. Kokoschka, Klee, Barlach, Arp are a few of the distinguished visual artists of the decade who, like Schiele, were also eminent as poets or playwrights. The poet Else Lasker-Schüler illustrated her own books, and it was to her that Franz Marc addressed his delightful picture postcard compositions. Almost all the leading writers of the decade were drawn or painted by sympathetic contemporaries. Egon Schiele's portraits of the painter and novelist A. P. Gütersloh and of the poet Karl Otten are cases in point, and other notable portraits of poets were produced by Kokoschka, Lehmbruck, Barlach and Ludwig Meidner among others. The idea of the *Gesamtkunstwerk* of course, goes back to an earlier period and a different aesthetic, but – in Austria especially – it remained fertile throughout the decade.

Yet the interpenetration of the arts, too, showed a curious overlapping of styles and affinities. In 1907 Erich Heckel was moved to produce a striking series of woodcuts not by the work of any experimental contemporary poet, but by Oscar Wilde's 'The Ballad of Reading Gaol'. For his early atonal songs the most radical of all the Austrian innovators in the arts, Arnold Schönberg, chose texts not by one of the younger modernist poets, not even by his Austrian contemporary Rilke – who was in sympathy with them and changed his style accordingly – but by Stefan George; and George's taste in typography and book illustration remained purely *art nouveau* to the end, the painter worshipped by George and his circle was Arnold Böcklin! Much in the same way Alban Berg based his operas on texts by Georg Büchner (1813–37!) and the pre-Expressionist, Frank Wedekind.

This brings us back to a peculiarly Austrian phenomenon already touched upon. A certain amount of such overlapping was inevitable everywhere. The pre-Dadaist German poems of Jean Arp, for instance, show an organic and significant debt to the imagery current in *art nouveau*, which was quite capable of producing a surrealism *avant la lettre*, a surrealism more decorative than subliminal. What is peculiarly Austrian is not this necessary transition from one mode to another but an almost deliberate reaching back for the past; not so much the sultry Viennese hyper-Romanticism of Schönberg's *Verklärte Nacht* as the introduction into Alban Berg's Violin Concerto of a Bach Chorale – with tremendous emotional effect. It was an Austrian, Hofmannsthal, who said that the 'powerful imagination is conservative'; and an Austrian poet, Franz Werfel, who managed to reconcile the stylistic innovations of the early Expressionists with a rhetoric that derives from Bach's contemporaries, the so-called Baroque poets.

Werfel was also an activist of the extreme left before becoming a Roman Catholic convert. The revolutionary impetus of that decade cut across all ideological divisions, as across all aesthetic ones, in its frenzied search for the new; but in every Austrian artist there is a strong pull towards tradition, and it is out of the tension between the two urges that the best Austrian artists of that decade created their works. Even Kafka took care to preserve much of the machinery of conventional fiction; without it, and without his dead-pan, functional prose style, his terrifyingly original fantasies would have lost not half, but all their power.

Egon Schiele's work, too, is unthinkable without the international adventurousness of the decade, its revolt against the old order in art and society, its longing for a *Menschheitsdämmerung*, the dawn of a new humanity. It is equally unthinkable without the Austrian urge to maintain a delicate balance of the old with the new, not to burn one's boats or make a clean sweep, but to remain receptive to many different promptings and possibilities, to keep the communications open in all directions.

Brecht and His Successors

FOR two hundred years or so the progress of European and American poetry was one towards autonomy. The more advanced the poet, the more his language differed from the language of discourse, exposition and plain talk. Not only metre, rhyme and metaphor served to remove poetry from those prosaic media of communication; more significantly still, the very syntax of poetry evolved in such a way that ambiguity or multiplicity of meaning came to be regarded as a distinguishing and essential feature of poetic utterance. The language of poetry, its practitioners and exegetes assumed, is unlike any other language. Far from being only a fine or memorable vehicle for thoughts, feelings or assertions that could be conveyed by other media, true poetry is at once the vehicle and the substance of its utterances; not a different way of putting things, but the only way of putting things that could not be said at all in any language but the language of poetry.

Non-specialists continue to complain of the peculiar difficulty or obscurity of modern poetry. Specialists continue to relish it, accepting Archibald MacLeish's dictum that 'a poem should not mean but be', while devoting long books and articles to the analysis of difficult poems and their dubious or multiple meanings. Yet at least one major twentieth-century poet, Bertolt Brecht, succeeded in writing a large and varied body of poetry that was clearly intended to convey a single meaning in language at least as plain and unfigurative as the best prose. Quite deliberately, Brecht set himself the aim of reversing the two-century old development which I have outlined. Since believers in the autonomy of poetry found it impossible to deny that Brecht was both a modern and a good poet, though his theory and practice alike contradicts their basic assumptions, many of them have found it prudent to ignore Brecht's poetry. Whether we see it as a revolution or as a counter-revolution, Brecht's achievement in poetry is not only remarkable in itself but inseparable from the survival of poetry after the Second World War, at least in those parts of the world in which the very foundations of autonomous poetry had been demolished by social and moral upheavals. If Brecht's later poetry is a kind of anti-poetry or minimal poetry, no other kind of poetry could withstand the anti-poetic fury of those who had seen European civilization reduced to a heap of rubble. It was Brecht's anticipation of this crisis that prompted him to 'wash' the language of poetry, as he put it, long before the crisis occurred; and what he washed out of poetry was nothing less than the sediment of the whole Romantic-Symbolist era, with its aesthetic of self-sufficiency. This revolution or counter-revolution was drastic enough to call for the attention of anyone interested in poetry.

Needless to say, Brecht's poetic development was bound up with his political and social concerns, which led him to identify the Romantic-Symbolist aesthetic with an order dominated by the bourgeoisie and by bourgeois individualism. Yet even among Marxist poets Brecht was very nearly alone in the radicalism with which he applied historical and sociological insights to the practice of poetry. His contemporary Johannes R. Becher, who became Minister of Culture in the German Democratic Republic, reacted against Expressionist obscurity, as Brecht did, but achieved no more by his language-washing than an old-fashioned banality of diction and a slackness of sentiment indistinguishable from that of the worst nineteenth-century versifiers. For a poet, ideology is not enough. To become effective in poetry the ideological commitment must enter his bloodstream like a food or a drug, pervading even his entrails and his dreams. Having done so, it becomes something other than mere ideology. That is why Brecht's later poems, for all their didacticism, can be appreciated and assimilated by non-Marxists, as Becher's later poems cannot.

Another way of putting it is that the Romantic-Symbolist in Brecht – and throughout the nineteen-twenties and early thirties he produced remarkable poems of a visionary, imaginatively autonomous kind – was not suppressed or silenced by an ideological decree but remained a dialectical presence beneath the hard, dry and spare surface of his later poems. The process of reduction was gradual, organic and total, involving the whole man. It began with the projection of an image, that of the tough, urban, proletarian poet dramatized in the early Villonesque poem 'Vom Armen B.B.':

> ... In der Asphaltstadt bin ich daheim. Von allem Anfang
> Versehen mit jedem Sterbsakrament:

Mit Zeitungen. Und Tabak. Und Branntwein.
Misstrauisch und faul und zufrieden am End.

Ich bin zu den Leuten freundlich. Ich setze
Einen steifen Hut auf nach ihrem Brauch.
Ich sage: es sind ganz besonders riechende Tiere,
Und ich sage: es macht nichts, ich bin es auch.

In meine leeren Schaukelstühle vormittags
Setze ich mitunter ein paar Frauen,
Und ich betrachte sie sorglos und sage ihnen:
In mir habt ihr einen, auf den könnt ihr nicht bauen . . .

. . . In the asphalt city I'm at home. From the very start
Provided with every unction and sacrament:
With newspapers. And tobacco. And brandy.
To the end mistrustful, lazy and content.

I'm polite and friendly to people. I put on
A stiff hat because that's what they do.
I say: they're animals with a quite peculiar smell
And I say: Does it matter? I am too.

Sometimes in the mornings on my empty rocking chairs
I'll sit a woman or two, and with an untroubled eye
Look at them steadily and say to them:
Here you have someone on whom you can't rely . . .

The later self-portraits, of which there are many, right up to
Brecht's last illness and the little poem in which he confronts his
imminent death, can do without the brashness and self-conscious
posturing of those lines, which were written as a provocation to the
bourgeoisie. In the later poems the toughness has become more than
a gesture, so that Brecht can also admit tenderness and gentleness,
just as he could admit that love of nature about which he tended to
feel uneasy, suspecting that it might be a residue of bourgeois self-
indulgence, aestheticism and idyllicism. Above all, in the later poems
he has ceased to care about himself as an individual; though he
draws freely on his own experience, even on his dreams, he is not
writing autobiography but availing himself of useful material for
reflections on the complexities of human motives and behaviour.
Here is one such poem, written in the thirties:

Fahrend in einem bequemen Wagen

Fahrend in einem bequemen Wagen
Auf einer regnerischen Landstrasse
Sahen wir einen zerlumpten Menschen bei Nachtanbruch
Der uns winkte, ihn mitzunehmen, sich tief verbeugend.
Wir hatten ein Dach und wir hatten Platz und wir fuhren vorüber
Und wir hörten mich sagen, mit einer grämlichen Stimme: Nein
Wir können niemand mitnehmen.
Wir waren schon weit voraus, einen Tagesmarsch vielleicht
Als ich plötzlich erschrak über diese meine Stimme
Dies mein Verhalten und diese
Ganze Welt.

Travelling in a Comfortable Car

Travelling in a comfortable car
Down a rainy road in the country
We saw a ragged fellow at nightfall
Signal to us for a ride, with a low bow.
We had a roof and we had room and we drove on
And we heard me say, in a morose tone of voice: No
We can't take anyone with us.
We had gone on a long way, perhaps a day's march
When suddenly I was shocked by this voice of mine
This behaviour of mine and this
Whole world.

This poem projects no image of Brecht as a poet or as a man that could distract us from his real concern with a general truth. The 'I' of the poem is confined to a strict function, which is impersonal. We are not asked to condemn Brecht's callousness or to grow mawkish over his remorse. We are asked to participate in the delayed shock at an action which could be and is anyone's. The poem has political as well as psychological implications, but the moral is not rubbed in or elaborated in ideological terms. It is enacted in terms of a simple occurrence simply told, yet without the simplification that would make it undialectical. The impersonality of Brecht's concern is brought out by the words, 'we heard me say' and by the concluding reference to 'this whole world'. One dialectical implication of the poem, that it is not enough to be a Marxist, as the reader knows

Brecht to be, would not have come across so forcefully if the first
person had been squeamishly excluded.

I say 'forcefully', though the little poem dispenses with all the
devices that serve to heighten the language of poetry for the sake of
eloquence, euphony or evocativeness. It dispenses with rhyme and
regular metre – though Brecht was a master of both in his earlier
verse – with alliteration and assonance, with metaphor and simile,
with inversions and dislocations of syntax. Brecht's art has come to
lie in the concealment of art, in a manner deliberately casual, throw-
away, undemonstrative. What distinguishes such poems from prose
is a rhythmic organization inconspicuous precisely because it is right,
perfectly accordant with what the poem says and enacts; and an
economy of means, a tautness and conciseness, that is rarely attained
in prose. By renouncing emotive effects and that vagueness which
Baudelaire considered an essential element in the beauty of Romantic
art, Brecht was able to create a didactic poetry that seems innocent
of any design on the reader, but all the more persuasive and convincing for that. Brecht's language here, once again, is anyone's
language, if anyone were capable of putting the right word in the
right place, of saying neither more nor less than he wants to say.
Brecht's ability to do so consistently, in hundreds of poems written
in this later manner, amounted to an achievement unique in his time,
the establishment of a new classicism. My allusion to Horace's words
about the concealment of art was no accident. To read Brecht's later
verse is an experience akin to the reading of Horace – whom Brecht
repeatedly read in his later years – the Catullus of the social epigrams
or any Latin poet at home not only in his art but in his world.

This does not mean that Brecht accepted his world uncritically,
any more than the Latin poets accepted theirs uncritically, but that
in Brecht's later poems personal and public concerns are inseparable.
The sequence of short poems which he called *Buckower Elegien*
(Buckow Elegies) – though by modern, non-classical standards they
are much closer to epigram than to elegy – was written after Brecht's
return to Germany, under a Communist régime, yet its dominant
tone is one of satirical and self-questioning unease, as in the opening
poem 'Der Radwechsel':

> Ich sitze am Strassenrand
> Der Fahrer wechselt das Rad.
> Ich bin nicht gern, wo ich herkomme.
> Ich bin nicht gern, wo ich hinfahre.

Warum sehe ich den Radwechsel
Mit Ungeduld?

Changing the Wheel

I sit on the roadside verge
The driver changes the wheel.
I do not like the place I have come from
I do not like the place I am going to.
Why with impatience do I
Watch him changing the wheel?

I have said that Brecht's late manner dispenses with metaphor and
simile, and so it does, except in so far as idiomatic usage is intrinsically figurative. Yet the very reduction of means in this short poem,
its extreme spareness and plainness of diction, invites us to read
more into it than it says, to read it as an allegory. Since self-projection
and self-expression are not what we look for in Brecht's later poems,
the extension of meaning we are likely to provide in this instance is
of a political or historical order; and however we interpret them, the
implications of the poem are very far from the optimism encouraged,
if not positively enforced, under Communist régimes. Several other
poems in the sequence quite unambiguously disparage or censure
this official optimism. The impatience in 'Changing the Wheel' has
little to do with it, though it could be related to Ernst Bloch's
'principle of hope', which can and must survive even when we know
and face up to the worst. This is the theme of another of the *Buckow
Elegies*, 'Die Wahrheit einigt' ('Truth unites us').

If the dialectic of 'Der Radwechsel' hides some of its implications
between the lines, leaving room for speculation and extensions of
meaning, other poems in the sequence could not be more explicit in
their insistence on truthfulness – truthfulness in the dealings between
government and subjects in 'Die Lösung' ('The Solution'), truthfulness about moral complexities, including the poet's own, in 'Böser
Morgen' ('A Bad Morning').

The accusing fingers of working men, in the last-named poem,
and the poet's guilty conscience deflected into a counter-accusation
of ignorance, point forward to Brecht's successors in the German
Democratic Republic no less than does his insistence on truthfulness,
on intellectual and moral rigour, and on a manner austere to the

point of self-effacement – though Brecht's later manner was as distinctive and unmistakable as that of any poet writing in his time. Compared to poets who grew up under the régime which accorded Brecht a privileged position, he had little reason to doubt that the freedom of literature was compatible with corporative needs on the one hand, government directives on the other. Towards the end of his life he could write the poem

Ich benötige keinen Grabstein

Ich benötige keinen Grabstein, aber
Wenn ihr einen für mich benötigt
Wünschte ich, es stünde darauf:
Er hat Vorschläge gemacht. Wir
Haben sie angenommen.
Durch eine solche Inschrift wären
Wir alle geehrt.

I Need No Gravestone

I need no gravestone, but
If you need one for me
I wish the inscription would read:
He made suggestions. We
Have acted on them.
Such an epitaph would
Honour us all.

Writing from more recent experience of the relations between intellectuals and government in East Germany, Professor Hans Mayer has remarked on the arrogance of Brecht's assumptions in that poem. Whether or not they are arrogant, Brecht's assumptions here are certainly different from those of his younger successors, who would not dare to suppose for one moment that the rulers of their country might feel honoured to take their advice. Brecht's confidence in that regard – a confidence essential to what I have called the classicism of his art – goes back to an earlier phase of revolutionary enterprise, when it did seem that independent thought and vision would be allowed to make a real contribution to the shaping of a new, socialist order. After Brecht's death that con-

fidence, or that arrogance, became the prerogative of those who were
not his successors, of the unthinking, unintelligent and uncritical
purveyors of authorized party pep to the people. It is language that
marks the difference, palpably and immediately: the language of
Brecht's successors is hard, spare, precise like his own, cryptic only
by omission and reduction, the language of the conformists is vague,
abstract, inflated, turgid with all the poeticisms which Brecht had
washed and scrubbed out of the texture of verse. The following
lines, written shortly before his death, show that Brecht was quite
aware of the risk he had taken by offering plain bread where others
offered cream puffs:

Und ich dachte immer

Und ich dachte immer: die allereinfachsten Worte
Müssen genügen. Wenn ich sage, was ist
Muss jedem das Herz zerfleischt sein.
Dass du untergehst, wenn du dich nicht wehrst
Das wirst du doch einsehn.

And I Always Thought

And I always thought: the very simplest words
Must be enough. When I say what things are like
Everyone's heart must be torn to shreds.
That you'll go down if you don't stand up for yourself –
Surely you see that.

Even these laconic and sad lines require an effort of imagination
and intelligence on the reader's part, a filling in of the gaps in their
dialectic, beginning with the gap bridged by the casual 'and' with
which the poem begins. One thing the gaps tell us, but the words do
not, is that Brecht must have had cause to question the effectiveness
of his simple words, precisely because too many of his readers had
been too thoroughly brainwashed to respond to his language-
washing. The brainwashing was to continue with a vengeance after
Brecht's death. The greater part of his large poetic output is available only in West Germany. That plain fact can be left to speak for
itself about the official response to poems that confine themselves to
saying 'what things are like'.

Brecht's successors, therefore, have had to take over his function of truth-telling without so much as a glimmer of hope that this function would be honoured by public approval, let alone by such reciprocal usefulness as Brecht claimed for writers in 'I Need No Gravestone'. Many of them have been tormented by serious and recurrent doubts as to the propriety of writing poetry at all under a system that denies all value to the individual conscience, the individual voice. After devoting much of his energy to the making of a diction free from the accretions of bourgeois individualism, Brecht had been able to strike a classical balance between private and public concerns, as his liberal use of the first person singular attests. (The index to his Collected Poems lists nearly eighty poems that begin with the word 'I'. That quite a number of these poems are written in persons other than his own confirms the importance which he attributed to personal experience as the only reliable means of enacting general truths.) In the work of younger East German poets that balance is upset once more, because the relationship between private and corporative needs has become dubious, critical and precarious.

A New Year stocktaking poem by Peter Gosse (born 1938) contains these lines:

> . . . Drei Jahre, zwei Pfund Lyrik,
> während mein Staat schuftet und schwitzt.
> Schluss mit der Kindheit.
> Ich werde exportreife Radars mitbaun,
> werde Mehrprodukt machen,
> werde mitmischen.

> . . . Three years, two pounds of verse,
> while my country drudges and sweats.
> Put an end to childhood.
> I shall help to make radars for export,
> shall help to increase productivity,
> shall mix in the mixing.

The realistic diction of this poem, 'Inventur Sylvester 64', is close enough to Brecht's to bring us up with a shock against the loss of nerve exemplified in the literal weighing up of the poet's output over the years. This materialism has ceased to be dialectical, even if we give the poet credit for a certain irony not made explicit in the rather

crude structure of this poem. Yet, ironic or not, the bad conscience
in the poem is real and widespread among the younger East German
poets. The accusing fingers that pointed at Brecht in a nightmare
have become a familiar and inescapable presence in waking life.

For all its plainness and colloquialism, Brecht's poetic language
was a distillation made from a great variety of components, literary
and historical as well as current. Gosse's diction, at least in the
passage quoted, is mimetic in its resort to contemporary jargon. It
is the contrast between his practice here and in other poems, which
are verbally idiosyncratic to the point of mannerism, that leads one
to suspect an ironic or satirical substratum which he may not have
intended.

There is no suspicion of irony about a short poem by Kurt
Bartsch (born 1937) that also relates the writing of poems to the
national economy, in terms less extreme and more Brechtian than
Gosse's:

poesie

die männer im elektrizitätswerk
zünden sich die morgenzigarette an.
sie haben, während ich nachtsüber schrieb,
schwitzend meine arbeitslampe gefüttert.
sie schippten Kohle für ein mondgedicht.

poetry

the men at the power station
light their morning cigarettes.
while I was writing at night
sweating they fed my work lamp.
they shovelled coal for a moon poem.

Brecht's direct lineage is as evident in this poem's language as in its
form. Its compressed dialectic is rendered in terms of factual
observation, not of abstract generalities. Inferences are left open, so
that the poem can be read as the discovery of a happy interdependence
between poetic and manual labour, or as a condemnation of poetry
for being parasitical on the exertions of working men. If the scales
are weighted towards the latter interpretation, it is only by the single

word 'moon'; and since Bartsch does not write 'moon poems' but poems of social awareness, the word was chosen because it heightens the dialectic and the poem's unemphatic play on contrasting sources of energy and light. Moon poems, the undialectical materialist will object, are useless to those useful men; but so are the cigarettes which they light all the same. The questions left open by those five brief lines could be debated at indefinite and boring length. One reason why Brecht's short later poems proved such a fruitful precedent for younger poets is that, even in East Germany, such poems cannot be expected to debate or answer all the questions they raise; and that is a distinct advantage under ideological censorship.

Brecht's contractions and reductions, in fact, have been carried farther by several of his successors, as by Günter Kunert (born 1929), whose early poetry is like a continuation of Brecht's in its moral searchingness and its epigrammatic sharpness. It is the reader who has to fill in the background of this little poem, 'Unterschiede', and any reader with first-hand experience of totalitarian systems will know how to fill it in:

> Betrübt höre ich einen Namen aufrufen:
> Nicht den meinigen.

> Aufatmend
> Höre ich einen Namen aufrufen:
> Nicht den meinigen.

> *Differences*

> Distressed, I hear a name called out:
> Not mine.

> Relieved,
> I hear a name called out:
> Not mine.

Apart from making a point about vanity and fear, what this poem enacts by its sparseness of diction and gesture is that sparseness has become the precondition of survival – the survival of truthful poetry and of truthful poets. The 'I' of this poem is incomparably more depersonalized than Brecht's, because it has been stripped not only of idiosyncrasy but circumstance. Where his concern is the survival

not of the individual but of the species, as in his poem 'Laika',
Kunert can be a little more circumstantial; but 'Laika' has the same
terse structure, based on parallelism like the other short poem, and
packed into a single sentence:

> In einer Kugel aus Metall,
> Dem besten, das wir besitzen,
> Fliegt Tag für Tag ein toter Hund
> Um unsre Erde
> Als Warnung,
> Dass so einmal kreisen könnte
> Jahr für Jahr um die Sonne,
> Beladen mit einer toten Menschheit,
> Der Planet Erde,
> Der beste, den wir besitzen.

> *Laika*

> In a capsule of metal,
> The best that we have,
> Day after day around our Earth
> A dead dog rotates
> As a warning
> That so in the end
> With a cargo of human corpses
> Year after year around the sun
> This planet Earth could rotate,
> The best that we have.

In other poems Kunert resorts to allegory or fable for relief from
the dual pressure of external and internal censorship; for the almost
self-effacing austerity of the kind of poems I have quoted is due to
the poet's conscience as much as to the repression of independent
thought.

This can be seen most clearly in the work of Reiner Kunze (born
1933), a subtle, witty and fearless critic of bureaucracy and repression, as in his fable 'Der Hochwald erzieht seine Bäume':

> Der hochwald erzieht seine bäume

> Sie des lichtes entwöhnend, zwingt er sie,
> all ihr grün in die kronen zu schicken

Die fähigkeit,
mit allen zweigen zu atmen,
das talent,
äste zu haben nur so aus freude,
verkümmern

Den regen siebt er, vorbeugend
der leidenschaft des durstes

Er lässt die bäume grösser werden
wipfel an wipfel:
Keiner sieht mehr als der andere,
dem wind sagen alle das gleiche

Holz

The Timber Forest Educates Its Trees

The timber forest educates its trees

By weaning them from light compels them
to send all their green into their tops
The ability
to breathe with every bough,
the talent
of having branches for the sheer joy of it
are stunted

The forest filters rain, as a precaution
against the passion of thirst

Lets the trees grow taller
crest to crest:
None sees more than another,
to the wind all tell the same thing

Wood

The fable here does not liberate the poet from his self-imposed austerity, since it serves only to convey something which he would not be allowed to say without it; and since this something is the utter drabness of conformity, a conformity imposed and enforced, the language too must not depart from drabness. Kunze has no illusions about the transparency of the disguise. Another of his poems is called 'Das Ende der Fabeln' ('The End of Fables').* In fairy-tale guise it shows why fables – and fairy-tales with a moral such as this one – are now dangerous:

> Es war einmal ein fuchs . . .
> beginnt der hahn
> eine fabel zu dichten
>
> Da merkt er
> so geht's nicht
> denn hört der fuchs die fabel
> wird er ihn holen

> Once upon a time there was a fox . . .
> the rooster begins
> to make up a fable
>
> But realizes
> it can't be done like that
> for if the fox hears the fable
> he'll come and get him

So much for outer censorship, which Kunze has continued to oppose and satirize in full consciousness of the risks involved. But inner censorship can be even more constricting, since it nags the poet with constant reminders that even his defiance will change nothing. Reiner Kunze has also written a poem that positively dissolves itself into silence and blankness, making all the crucial connections between minimal poetry, minimal language, and the shrinking space occupied by the individual where the 'collective' is worshipped as an omnipotent deity:

> *Entschuldigung*
>
> Ding ist ding
> sich selbst genug
>
> Überflüssig
> das zeichen

* For the complete texts of this poem, see *East German Poetry*, ed. Michael Hamburger, Carcanet, 1972, pp. 122–3.

Überflüssig
das wort

(überflüssig
ich)

Apology

A thing's a thing
sufficient to itself

superfluous
the sign

superfluous
the word

(superfluous
I)

The elliptical syntax of that poem – as opposed to the regular and logical syntax of Brecht – serves to avoid the presumption of statement, of assertion. This is poetry with its back against the wall, uttering the barest of dispensable words to bear witness still to the truth, though that truth is its own dispensability.

Reiner Kunze has written another fable called 'Das Ende der Kunst' ('The End of Art'), but the dialectic and paradox of poetry demand that even silence be articulated, even defeat and exasperation recorded. The danger of being silenced by force, like Wolf Biermann whom Kunze defended in a playful but unambiguous poem, has not deterred Kunze. He has written about that too, in a poem without a fable closely akin to Kunert's poem 'Differences':

Zimerlautstärke

Dann die
zwölf jahre
durfte ich nicht publizieren sagt
der mann im radio

Ich denke an X
und beginne zu zählen

Low Volume

Then for
twelve years
I was forbidden to publish
says the man on the radio

I think of X
and start counting

The implied analogy with a writer silenced under National Socialism makes this the most daring of all Kunze's poems in defence of freedom. Yet his minimal language has preserved him from the blatant and outraged defiance of the collective expressed in Wolf Biermann's poem 'Rücksichtslose Schimpferei' ('All-in Tirade'), with its opening assertion *Ich ich ich*. Not only this assertion of the personal principle but his preference for Villonesque ballads and pop song lyrics brings Biermann closer to the position of the early pre-Marxist Brecht than any of his East German contemporaries, though even this defiant and exasperated poem contains an admission of personal fallibility, and Biermann too has a place in the later Brecht's succession. With a charm and a lightness of touch peculiar to him he employs minimal diction and epigrammatic trenchancy in this short poem:

ACH FREUND, GEHT ES NICHT AUCH DIR SO?
ich kann nur lieben
      was ich die Freiheit habe
         auch zu verlassen:

dieses Land
diese Stadt
diese Frau
dieses Leben

Eben darum lieben ja
wenige ein Land
manche eine Stadt

viele eine Frau
aber alle das Leben.

OH, FRIEND, DON'T YOU FIND IT'S THE SAME WITH YOU?
I can only love
    what I am also free
        to leave:

this country
this city
this woman
this life

And that's the reason why
so few love a country
some love a city
many love a woman
but all love life.

A great many more poets and poems could be cited in this context; and Brecht's successors include West German poets, as well as East European poets writing in languages other than German. Brevity in itself does not necessarily answer the same needs and intentions as those with which I have been concerned. In America, for instance, oriental forms like the *haiku* – which also influenced Brecht – have been cultivated for purposes quite different from those of Brecht or his successors, giving prominence to the very autonomous image which Brecht virtually banished from his later verse.

Historically, the whole phenomenon of minimal language in poetry may be no more than a freak, at least in its later, post-Brechtian phase. Poetry has always tended towards compression, so much so that Ezra Pound wanted the German word 'dichten' – to make poetry – to be derived from the adjective 'dicht' – dense – which etymologically it is not. But Brecht's diction was not particularly dense or condensed. Except where he was cryptic, deliberately so, for good and cunning reasons, his plain language was logical and relaxed, minimal only in its avoidance of ornament, of emotive devices, of the inwardness cultivated by Romantics and Symbolists. What Brecht wanted, and would have achieved if political developments had not forbidden it, was a social poetry of dialogue about matters of interest to everyone. This eminently classical relationship between writer and reader had long been made impossible by the individualism of writers and readers alike, and nowhere more so than in serious and advanced poetry, with its need to escape from vulgar norms of communication in every conceivable direction. Brecht, therefore, undertook a drastic and rigorous revision of the function of poetry and of poets so as to put both back where he thought they belonged, in society and in history.

Brecht's successors, Marxists like him, accepted his premisses and wanted to work along the same lines; but the freedom granted to Brecht as a special cultural asset was not granted to them. Far from welcoming the advice and criticism of poets whose social and moral awareness did not turn them into conformists, such poets were grudgingly tolerated at best, publicly disgraced or silenced at the worst. The more repressive those authorities who claimed to represent the will of the masses, the more poets were forced to question the reality of this so-called collective. The very medium which Brecht had evolved for plain speaking in poetry became the last remaining receptacle for frantic messages so abbreviated as to be almost as cryptic as the hermetic poetry which it had replaced. To carry that development any farther would amount to self-imposed silence, and thus to defeat. It is likely, therefore, that poetry will have to put on flesh again, as it has in the work of other young East German poets like Volker Braun and Karl Mickel, and in the later work of Günter Kunert, all of whom have also begun to draw more freely than minimal poetry permitted on immediate personal experience, not only of the socially exemplary kind.

Even in its extreme reduction – dispensable words set down by dispensable poets – minimal poetry should remain of interest as an instance of the extraordinary resilience of poetic language, its power to survive and function when it was little more than a skeleton, stripped of all the sensuous appeal traditionally associated with it. Though by omission, ellipsis, disguise, it managed to tell the truth about itself and about society, when no other medium could do so. When outer and inner pressures forbade the free play of imagination, of feeling and of perception, its very austerity and reticence served to uphold that freedom, by reminding us of its loss. Unlike some of the protest poetry written in other circumstances, it cannot be dismissed as a form of self-indulgence, since it admitted no personal idiosyncrasy, no expansive gesture, no intoxicating or intoxicated rhetoric; and it was written by men who had no illusions about the effectiveness of protest in poetry, but knew only too well that those in power would not honour them, or honour themselves, by taking the advice of poets. Yet by a self-effacement that was also political self-exposure they protested none the less. If, by another dialectical twist, that desperate defiance points back to the fundamental autonomy of poetic language, it is as well to remember that even so committed a poet as Brecht granted that 'art is an autonomous realm', though as a Marxist he distinguished this necessary autonomy from what he called autarchy. In their own way, and in an extremity more constricting than Brecht's, his successors remained true both to their art and to their commitments beyond art. If only for that, their minimal poetry will be remembered.

Johannes Bobrowski:
An Introduction

BOBROWSKI is no more a typical East German poet than Grass is a typical West German poet. Both were born on the Eastern fringes of the then German-speaking territories, both were of mixed German and Slav descent, both grew up in an ethnic borderland that was a meeting-place and melting-pot of cultures and peoples. As soon as we turn from their poetry to their prose – and Bobrowski, too, was a novelist and short story writer – their common preoccupations become as striking as their differences. In their prose fiction, at any rate, Bobrowski and Grass show a common concern with this particular borderland, its way of life, its conflicts and tensions, even its legends and myths, down to the pagan sub-stratum of ancient Prussian lore. Oscar's 'two Fathers', the German and the Polish, in Grass's *The Tin Drum*, are an extreme instance of this writer's imaginative involvement with the city in which he grew up. Bobrowski's allegiances and sympathies extended to many non-German peoples of Eastern Europe, including Lithuanians, Poles, Russians, Gypsies and Jews. One distinction of all his work is that it celebrates this vanished world of village or small-town communities in an incomparably vivid and poignant way.

Johannes Bobrowski was born in Tilsit, East Prussia, on 9 April 1917. He attended school in Königsberg and began to study History of Art before being called up. His first poems were written, but not published, when he was a soldier in Russia in 1941. Soon after, he was taken prisoner by the Russians and did not return to Germany until 1949, when he settled in East Berlin, working as a publisher's reader. A few of his poems appeared in East German periodicals in the fifties, but it was in 1960 that his work was introduced to West German readers in the anthology *Deutsche Lyrik auf der anderen Seite*. Between 1960 and 1965 he published two books of poems, a novel, and two books of short stories. All of them appeared both in

West and East German editions, winning distinguished literary prizes in East Germany, West Germany and Switzerland. On 2 September 1965 Johannes Bobrowski died in Berlin, at the age of forty-eight. A second novel was published posthumously in 1966, and he prepared a third collection of poems, *Wetterzeichen*, before his sudden illness – acute appendicitis complicated by septicaemia – and his premature death.

Very little of Bobrowski's poetry is directly autobiographical or confessional. Yet he was a deeply committed poet, and his deep moral commitment was so important to him that he regarded his own person and circumstances as relatively unimportant. A very unusual degree of self-effacement was essential to what he had to say, as it was to his character as a man. Had he been less of an artist, didacticism might have been a dangerous temptation, but his poetry and his shorter prose works are almost as free of didacticism as they are of self-display. If we want to know what his commitment was, in explicit and unambiguous terms, we have to refer to his novel *Levins Mühle* or to this little note contributed to an anthology:

> I began to write near Lake Ilmen in 1941, about the Russian land-scape, but as a foreigner, a German. This became a theme – something like this: the Germans and the European East – because I grew up around the river Memel, where Poles, Lithuanians, Russians and Germans lived together and, amid them all, the Jews – a long story of unhappiness and guilt, for which my people is to blame, ever since the days of the Order of Teutonic Knights. Not to be undone, perhaps, or expiated, but worthy of hope and honest endeavour in German poems. I have been helped in this by the example of a master: Klopstock.

The impersonality of Bobrowski's poems, then, has to do with his sense of being dedicated to a special task – to expiate the guilt of which he speaks in the note; and this guilt was not personal either. Klopstock was only one of the many masters and mentors to whom he turned for support. He was familiar with many languages and literatures, and his poems about writers and artists as various as Villon, Góngora and Dylan Thomas show the same power of self-identification as his poems about landscapes and places. In every case it is the place or the person evoked that matters, not Bobrowski himself or his opinions and circumstances. When he does write about himself, he does so with an extraordinary spareness and humility, as in these lines from the poem 'Absage':

> I am a man,
> one flesh with his wife,
> who raises his children
> for an age without fear.

This is one of the few personal statements which Bobrowski permitted himself in the poems – and its bareness is such as to make it impersonal. Another occurs in a late poem, 'Sprache', in which he characterizes his own poetic language as 'being on its interminable way to my neighbour's house'. 'Out of time's not far to go', Bobrowski wrote in 'Village Music', one of the many poems in which he anticipates his own death, and one of the few that show his debt to another tradition, the tradition of folk song. All his poetry moves in a dimension much larger than biographical or historical time, between things he had himself seen in Eastern Europe and the mythical world of folklore, both German and Balto-Slav.

The rhythmic and syntactic structure of Bobrowski's poems is as unmistakably personal as his themes and diction are impersonal. Unlike most German poets of his time he could afford to borrow from the vocabulary of older poetic conventions; and such borrowings were necessary, since they serve to relate the historical occasions of his poems to the other dimension of time which they explore. The halting and elliptic syntax of Bobrowski's poems enacts the difficult stages of that exploration. In the same way his rhythmic allusions to ode and elegy forms are used to create a suspense and distance peculiar to his work.

Bobrowski's modernity is as unobtrusive as all his other virtues. Only a poet deeply involved in the issues and disasters of our time could have written those poems, but their uniqueness owes less to immediate experience, immediate observation, than to Bobrowski's capacity to span great distances – geographical, temporal and cultural – and yet to be wholly present everywhere.

Moralist and Jester: The Poetry of Günter Grass

WHEN I ask myself what makes Günter Grass so outstanding a phenomenon as a poet, the first answer that occurs to me is: the circumstance that he is so many other things as well, an outstanding novelist, playwright, draughtsman, politician and cook. In an age of specialists such diversity of interest and accomplishment could well be suspect, as indeed it is to some of Günter Grass's critics. Yet the more one looks at Grass's diverse activities the more clearly one sees that they all spring from the same source and centre; also, that the unfashionable diversity is inseparable from his achievement in each of these, and other, fields, because the whole man moves together, within the area of his dominant tensions and concerns. I am far from wanting to claim that this area, in Günter Grass's case, is unlimited; but it is strikingly and decisively larger than that of most other poets in our time, and that is one reason why Günter Grass's poetry is so difficult to place in terms of literary history, trends and genres.

In the early nineteen-fifties, when Grass was writing the poems collected in his first book, *Die Vorzüge der Windhühner*, Gottfried Benn was still advocating what he called 'absolute poetry', 'words assembled in a fascinating way' and not subject to moral or social criteria. On the other hand, and on the other side, Bertolt Brecht was still advocating a kind of poetry to be judged by its moral and social usefulness. Benn's emphasis was on self-expression, the enacting of inner states; Brecht's on the rendering of external and communal realities. If we ask ourselves to which of these sides Günter Grass belonged as a poet – and almost all the better poetry written by German writers of Grass's generation follows a line of development that can be traced back to that crucial divergence – we come up against one aspect of Grass's capacity to embrace and balance extreme opposites. Shortly after the publication of *Die Vorzüge der Windhühner* Grass wrote three short prose pieces which appeared in the periodical *Akzente* under the title 'Der Inhalt als Widerstand' ('Content as Resistance'), in which imagination and reality, fantasy and observation, are treated not as alternatives but as the generators of a necessary tension. The middle piece, a brief dramatic account of a walk taken by two poets, Pempelfort and Krudewil, presents the extreme alternatives. Pempelfort is in the habit of stuffing himself with indigestible food before going to bed, to induce nightmares and genitive metaphors which he can jot down between fits of sleep; the quoted specimens of his poems place him in the line of development which includes German Expressionism and the Surrealism that was rediscovered by German poets after the war. Krudewil, on the other hand, wants to 'knit a new Muse', who is 'grey, mistrustful and totally dreamless, a meticulous housewife'. This homely and matter-of-fact Muse points to the practice of Brecht, who drew on dreams not for metaphors or images, but moralities. Grass's treatment of these two characters is good-humouredly and humorously impartial. Those who misunderstand Grass's moderation, and moderation generally, as either indifference or weakness, when it is the strength of those who don't lose their heads in a crisis, could regard this piece as an early instance of Grass's equivocation; but Grass would not have bothered to write the dialogue if he had not been deeply involved in the issues which it raises.

Before turning to Grass's poems I want to touch on one other prose piece, published nearly ten years later in the same periodical, when Grass had become a celebrated writer and a controversial public figure. It is the lecture 'Vom mangelnden Selbstvertrauen der schreibenden Hofnarren unter Berücksichtigung nicht vorhandener Höfe' ('On the Lack of Self-confidence among Writing Court Fools in View of Non-existent Courts'). The very title, with its baroque and ironic identification of writers with court fools, was an affront to the solemn self-righteousness of the new radicals, who disapproved not only of Grass's incorrigible addiction to clowning in his verse and prose fiction but also of his commitment to a political party more evolutionary than revolutionary, a party guilty of moderation and compromise. What is more, Grass came out in favour of a position half-way between what the radicals understood by commitment – the subordination of art to political and social programmes – and the essential demand of art itself for free play of the imagination, the freedom which Grass identifies with that of the court fool or jester. If a writer is worried about the state of affairs in his country and elsewhere, Grass argues – and there can be no doubt at all that Grass himself cares about it passionately – the best way to do something about it is the way of political action proper – the kind of action which Grass himself has undertaken on behalf of the political party which he supports. As for his writing, if it is imaginative writing, he should resist every kind of extraneous pressure that would transform it into a vehicle or weapon. 'Poems admit of no compromises; but we live by compromises. Whoever can endure this tension every day of his life is a fool and changes the world.'

In practice, of course – and in literature as much as in practical politics or in cooking – it isn't a matter of this or that, but a little more of this rather than a little more of that; not of imagination or reality, of clowning or didacticism, of commitment or non-commitment, but of a particular proportion in every instance that makes for rightness. Because he bears this in mind at all times, in everything to which he applies himself, Grass is not only an anti-specialist but an anti-ideologist. Even his theoretical pronouncements are nourished and sustained by his awareness of complexity, an awareness which he owes to first-hand experience. In his imaginative works, including his poems, the mixture has not remained constant. Just as in his prose fiction there has been a gradual shift away from subjective fantasy to observed realities, a shift parallelled in his plays, it is the first book of poems that shows Grass at his most exuberantly and uninhibitedly clownish. This is not to say that these early poems lack moral or metaphysical seriousness, but that the element of free play in them is more pronounced and more idiosyncratic than in the later poems, in which the clown has to defend his privilege of freedom, a special freedom begrudged to him by the moralist and the politician.

It has become something of a commonplace in Grass criticism to note that his imagination and invention are most prolific where he is closest to childhood experience, by which I mean both his own, as evoked in the more or less autobiographical sections of *Die Blechtrommel* and *Katz und Maus* or in the more or less autobiographical poem 'Kleckerburg', and childish modes of feeling, seeing and behaving. Almost without exception, the poems in Grass's first book owe their vigour and peculiarity to this mode of feeling, seeing, and behaving. These early poems enact primitive gestures and processes without regard for the distinctions which adult rationality imposes on the objects of perception. They have their being in a world with-

out divisions or diştinctions, full of magical substitutions and transformations. To speak of surrealism in connection with those early
poems tells us little about them, because they are as realistic as they
are fantastic, with a realism that seems fantastic only because it is
true to the polymorphous vision of childhood. As far as literary
influences are concerned, Grass's early poems are far less closely
related to the work of any Surrealist poet than to that of a Dadaist,
Jean (or Hans) Arp, whose eye and ear had the same mischievous
innocence, giving a grotesque twist to everyday objects and banal
phrases. In his later, post-Dadaist work, Arp also adapted his unanchored images and metaphors to increasingly moral and social
preoccupations, not to mention the metaphysical ones which, much
like Grass, he had always combined with his comic zest.

Most of the poems in *Die Vorzüge der Windhühner* deal in unanchored images, like the 'eleventh finger' which cannot be tied
down to any particular plane of meaning or symbolism, but owes its
genesis and function to a complex of largely personal associations.
Such unanchored and floating images were also carried over into
Grass's prose, especially in *Die Blechtrommel*, and some of them had
such obsessional power over Grass's imagination that they recur
with variations in his poems, prose narratives, plays and drawings.
(Dolls, nuns, cooks and hens are a few of those I have in mind. In
many cases these, in turn, are associated with processes – such as
flying, in the case of nuns – which are even more important to Grass
than the thing, person or animal itself.) The substitution practised
by Grass in these poems also includes drastic synaesthesia, as in the
many poems connected with music, orchestras, musical instruments.
Sounds are freely transposed into visual impressions and vice versa,
as in 'Die Schule der Tenöre' ('The School for Tenors'):

> Nimm den Lappen, wische den Mond fort,
> schreibe die Sonne, die andere Münze
> über den Himmel, die Schultafel.
> Setze dich dann.
> Dein Zeugnis wird gut sein,
> du wirst versetzt werden,
> eine neue, hellere Mütze tragen.
> Denn die Kreide hat recht
> und der Tenor der sie singt.
> Er wird den Samt entblättern,
> Efeu, Meterware der Nacht,

Moos, ihren Unterton,
jede Amsel wird er vertreiben.

Den Bassisten, mauert ihn ein
in seinem Geölbe.
Wer glaubt noch an Fässer
in denen der Wein fällt?
Ob Vogel oder Schrapnell,
oder nur Summen bis es knackt,
weil der Äther überfüllt ist
mit Wochenend und Sommerfrische.
Scheren, die in den Schneiderstuben
das lied von Frühling und Konfektion zwitschern, –
hieran kein Beispiel.

Die Brust heraus, bis der Wind seinen Umweg macht.
Immer wieder Trompeten,
spitzgedrehte Tüten voller silberner Zwiebeln.
Dann die Geduld.
Warten bis der Dame die Augen davonlaufen,
zwei unzufriedene Dienstmädchen.
Jetzt erst den Ton den die Gläser fürchten
und der Staub
der die Gesimse verfolgt bis sie hinken.

Fischgräten, wer singt diese Zwischenräume,
den Mittag, mit Schilf gespiesst?
Wie schön sang Else Fenske, als sie,
während der Sommerferien,
in grosser Höhe danebentrat,
in einen stillen Gletscherspalt stürzte,
und nur ihr Schirmchen
und das hohe C zurückliess.

Das hohe C, die vielen Nebenflüsse des Missisippi,
der herrliche Atem,
der die Kuppeln erfand und den Beifall.
Vorhang, Vorhang, Vorhang.
Schnell, bevor der Leuchter nicht mehr klirren will,
bevor die Galerien knicken
und die Seide billig wird.
Vorhang, bevor du den Beifall begreifst.

Take your duster, wipe away the moon,
write the sun, that other coin
across the sky, the blackboard.
Then take your seat.
Your report will be a good one,
you will go up one class,
wear a new, brighter cap.
For the chalk is in the right
and so is the tenor who sings it.
He will unroll the velvet,
ivy, yard-measured wares of night,
loss, its undertone,
every blackbird he'll drive away.

The bass – immure him
in his vault.
Who now believes in barrels
in which the wine-level falls?
Whether bird or shrapnel
or only a hum till it cracks
because the ether is overcrowded
with weekend and seaside resort.
Scissors which in the tailors' workshops
twitter the song of springtime and haute couture –
this is no example.

Puff out your chest, till the wind takes its devious way.
Trumpets again and again,
conical paper bags full of silver onions.
After that, patience.
Wait till the lady's eyes run away,
two dissatisfied skivvies.
Only now that tone which the glasses fear
and the dust
that pursues the ledges until they limp.

Fishbones, who will sing these gaps,
sing noon impaled with rushes?
How well did Elsie Fenner sing
when, in the summer vacation
at a great height she took a false step,
tumbled into a silent glacier crevasse
and left nothing behind but
her little parasol and the high C.

The high C, the many tributaries of the Mississippi,
the glorious breath
that invented cupolas and applause.
Curtain, curtain, curtain.
Quick, before the candelabrum refuses to jingle,
before the galleries droop
and silk becomes cheap.
Curtain, before you understand the applause.

I shall not attempt a lengthy interpretation of this poem which would amount to a translation of it into the terms of adult rationality – terms irrelevant to the poem, in any case. In my context it is enough to point out that its subject – or content, to link up with Grass's early contribution to poetics – is little more than a sequence of kinetic gestures, derived in the first place from a personal response to the singing of tenors, but proceeding by a series of free substitutions and transpositions. These substitutions and transpositions observe no distinctions between one order of experience and another, between aural and visual phenomena, between what is physically plausible and what is not. As in surrealist writing, metaphor is autonomous; but, though one thing in the poem leads to another by associations that are astonishingly fluid, the poem is held together by an organization different from automatic writing in that the initial phenomenon is never quite left behind. Ingenuity and intellectual invention, too, are part of that organization, as in metaphysical or baroque poetry. Hence the wit, akin to the conceits of seventeenth-century poets, which is essential to Grass's art. Grass avails himself of the freedom of polymorphous childishness; but since he is not a child, and even his poems of innocence include the awareness of experience, wit serves him as a necessary mediator between the conscious and the subconscious reservoirs that feed his art. The association of the bass voice, for instance, with a cellar, hence with wine and, most appropriately, with a wine barrel or vat in which the level falls, is so elementary as to be easily followed by anyone who has not lost all access to the sub-rational levels of his own mind. The likening of a tenor voice to 'conical paper bags full of silver onions' is a little more far-fetched, a little more ingenious, but just as convincing; and so is all the play on light and darkness, bright and sombre sounds, leading to the dynamic analogy of cutting cloth, to scissors, tailors and haute couture. Grass is at his most clownishly farcical in the passage introducing the woman singer who takes a false step, yet even her

plunge into the crevasse is consistent with the whole poem's trans-
sensory dynamism.

But for the wit and the more ingenious allusions in poems like
'The School for Tenors' they would belong to a realm of clown's and
child's play which is amoral and asocial. Yet even in 'The School for
Tenors' satirical implications arise from references to historical
phenomena like seaside resorts, shrapnel and, above all, to audiences
in an opera house. The very short, almost epigrammatic pieces in the
same collection present Grass the moralist looking over the shoulder
of the clown and child, not least incisively in 'Familiär' ('Family
Matters'), which has the additional irony of judging the adult world
from a child's point of view – a device most characteristic of the man
who was to write *The Tin Drum*, as well as later poems like 'Advent'.
Incidentally, 'Familiär' reminds us that Grass, a writer who has
been accused of obscenity, blasphemy and every conceivable affront
to the *bien-pensants*, was brought up as a Roman Catholic:

> In unserem Museum, – wir besuchen es jeden Sonntag, –
> hat man eine neue Abteilung eröffnet.
> Unsere abgetriebenen Kinder, blasse, ernsthafte Embryos,
> sitzen dort in schlichten Gläsern
> und sorgen sich um die Zukunft ihrer Eltern.

Family Matters

> In our museum – we always go there on Sundays –
> they have opened a new department.
> Our aborted children, pale, serious embryos,
> sit there in plain glass jars
> and worry about their parents' future.

Here the grey, meticulous Muse of everyday matters seems to
have taken over from the Muse of fantasy and dreams, as it was to
do – up to a point – in Grass's second and third books of poems.
Yet the epigrammatic and didactic impact is made through fantasy –
as in some of Arp's later poems – not through a consequential literalness, as practised by Brecht in short poems like the *Buckower
Elegien* and by Brecht's many successors in West and East Germany.
Very few of Grass's later poems are as exuberantly playful as most
of those in his first collection; but just as the moralist was not

wholly absent from the early poems, the clowning fantast and the polymorphous sensualist keep popping up in later poems seemingly dominated by political and social satire. The creative tension permits, and indeed demands, a good deal of movement in one direction; but it does not break.

In Grass's next collection, *Gleisdreieck*, it is the poems that touch on divided Berlin which give the clearest indication of how fantasy interlocks with minute observation in Grass's work. The elaborate documentation that preceded the writing of *The Tin Drum* is one instance of a development that can also be traced in the poems and the drawings, from the high degree of abstraction in the drawings done for *Die Vorzüge der Windhühner* to the grotesque magnification of realistic detail in the drawings done for *Gleisdreieck*, and on to the meticulous verisimilitude of the clenched hand reproduced on the cover of the third collection, *Ausgefragt*. Grass's growing involvement in politics is intimately bound up with that artistic development. The mainly personal and fantastic poem 'Ausverkauf' ('Sale') in *Gleisdreieck* contains this unmistakable allusion to East Berlin:

> Während ich alles verkaufte,
> enteigneten sie fünf oder sechs Strassen weiter
> die besitzanzeigenden Fürwörter
> und sägten den kleinen harmlosen Männern
> den Schatten ab, den privaten.

> While I was selling it all,
> five or six streets from here they expropriated
> all the possessive pronouns
> and sawed off the private shadows
> of little innocuous men.

The underlying seriousness of Grass's clowning – as of all good clowning – is even more evident in *Gleisdreieck* than in the earlier collection. Without any loss of comic zest or invention Grass can now write existential parables like 'Im Ei' ('In the Egg') or 'Saturn', poems that take the greater risk of being open to interpretation in terms other than those of pure zany fantasy. One outstanding poem in *Gleisdreieck* has proved utterly untranslatable, because its effect depends on quadruple rhymes and on corresponding permutations of meaning for which only the vaguest equivalents can be found in another language. Grass himself has a special liking for this poem, the sinister nursery rhyme 'Kinderlied', perhaps because it represents the most direct and the most drastic fusion in all his poetry of innocence and experience. This artistic fusion results from the confrontation of the freedom most precious to Grass, the freedom of child's play which is also the court jester's prerogative, with its polar opposite, the repression of individuality imposed by totalitarian political régimes.

> Wer lacht hier, hat gelacht?
> Hier hat sich's ausgelacht.
> Wer hier lacht, macht Verdacht,
> dass er aus Gründen lacht.
>
> Wer weint hier, hat geweint?
> Hier wird nicht mehr geweint.
> Wer hier weint, der auch meint,
> dass er aus Gründen weint.
>
> Wer spricht hier, spricht und schweigt?
> Wer schweigt, wird angezeigt.
> Wer hier spricht, hat verschwiegen,
> wo seine Gründe liegen.
>
> Wer spielt hier, spielt im Sand?
> Wer spielt muss an die Wand,
> hat sich beim Spiel die Hand
> gründlich verspielt, verbrannt.
>
> Wer stirbt hier, ist gestorben?
> Wer stirbt, ist abgeworben.
> Wer hier stirbt, unverdorben
> ist ohne Grund verstorben.

Laughing, weeping, talking, keeping silent, playing and even dying are the spontaneous and uncalculated actions to which totalitarian repression attributes subversive political motives, drowning 'the ceremony of innocence'. No other poem by Grass has the same combination of simplicity and intricacy, extreme economy of means and extreme wealth of implication. Apart from the taut syntactic structure and the rhyme scheme, the poem is untranslatable because no single word in English has the familiar and horrible connotations of a German word like 'angezeigt' – reported to the police or other official authority as being ideologically suspect – or 'abgeworben' –

the bureaucratic counterpart to being excommunicated, blackballed, expelled, deprived of civil rights, ceasing to exist as a member of a corporative and collective order that has become omnipotent. The same applies to the line 'Wer spielt muss an die Wand,' where 'having to go to the wall' means summary execution.

It is characteristic of the state of West German literature in the late sixties that Günter Grass's third collection of poems, *Ausgefragt*, gave rise to political controversies rather than to literary ones; and the collection does contain a relatively high proportion of poems that respond directly – perhaps too directly in some cases – to political and topical issues. Some of them, like 'In Ohnmacht gefallen' ('Powerless, with a Guitar'), were bound to be read as provocations or correctives aimed at the radical left:

> Wir lesen Napalm und stellen Napalm uns vor.
> Da wir uns Napalm nicht vorstellen können,
> lesen wir über Napalm, bis wir uns mehr
> unter Napalm vorstellen können.
> Jetzt protestieren wir gegen Napalm.
>   Nach dem Frühstück, stumm,
>   auf Fotos sehen wir, was Napalm vermag.
>   Wir zeigen uns grobe Raster
>   und sagen: Siehst du, Napalm.
>   Das machen sie mit Napalm.
> Bald wird es preiswerte Bildbände
> mit besseren Fotos geben,
> auf denen deutlicher wird,
> was Napalm vermag.
> Wir kauen Nägel und schreiben Proteste.
>   Aber es gibt, so lesen wir,
>   Schlimmeres als Napalm.
>   Schnell protestieren wir gegen Schlimmeres.
>   Unsere berechtigten Proteste, die wir jederzeit
>   verfassen falten frankieren dürfen, schlagen zu Buch.
> Ohnmacht, an Gummifassaden erprobt.
> Ohnmacht legt Platten auf: ohnmächtige Songs.
> Ohne Macht mit Guitarre, –
> Aber feinmaschig und gelassen
> wirkt sich draussen die Macht aus.

> We read napalm and imagine napalm.
> Since we cannot imagine napalm

we read about napalm until
by napalm we can imagine more.
Now we protest against napalm.
    After breakfast, silent,
    we see in photographs what napalm can do.
    We show each other coarse screen prints
    and say: there you are, napalm.
    They do that with napalm.
Soon there'll be cheap picture books
with better photographs
which will show more clearly
what napalm can do.
We bite our nails and write protests.
    But, we read, there are
    worse things than napalm.
    Quickly we protest against worse things.
    Our well-founded protests, which at any time
    we may compose fold stamp, mount up.
Impotence, tried out on rubber façades.
Impotence puts records on: impotent songs.
Powerless, with a guitar. –
But outside, finely meshed
and composed, power has its way.

Compared with Grass's earlier poems this one gives little scope
for playfulness. An almost Brechtian literalness and austerity seem
to contradict Grass's resolve to keep the court fool separate from the
politically committed citizen. Yet I think it would be wrong to read
this poem primarily as a polemic against the radicals. The gravity of
its manner suggests that Grass is quarrelling more with himself than
with others, that he is rendering a painful experience of his own.
The old exuberance re-asserts itself elsewhere in the same collection,
even in thematically related poems like 'Der Dampfkessel-Effekt'
('The Steam Boiler Effect') which *are* primarily polemical. As for the
trilogy 'Irgendwas machen' ('Do Something'), its centre piece 'Die
Schweinekopfsülze' ('The Jellied Pig's Head') was clearly intended
to be a sustained satirical analogy, but somehow the cook seems to
take over from the political satirist, deriving so much pleasure from
his recipe in its own right that the reader too is carried away from
politics to the kitchen. Perhaps the happiest poem of all in *Ausgefragt*
– happiest in two senses of the word – is 'Advent', since it blends
social satire with the freedom and zest which – in Grass's work –

appertain to the world of childhood. Even here, and in the autobiographical poem 'Kleckerburg', the tension has become extreme,
because the amorality of childhood is at once re-enacted and judged
in the light of mature social experience. 'Advent', in fact, juxtaposes
the war games of children and those both of their parents and of
nations:

> . . . wenn Onkel Dagobert wieder was Neues,
> die Knusper-Kneisschen-Maschine
> und ähnliche Mehrzweckwaffen Peng! auf den Markt wirft
> bis eine Stunde später Rickeraffe . . . Puff . . . Plops!
> der konventionelle, im Kinderzimmer lokalisierte Krieg
> sich unorthodox hochschaukelt,
> und die Eltern,
> weil die Weihnachtseinkäufe
> nur begrenzte Entspannung erlauben,
> und Tick, Track und Trick, –
> das sind Donald Ducks Neffen, –
> wegen nichts Schild und Schwert vertauscht haben,
> ihre gegenseitige, zweite und abgestufte,
> ihre erweiterte Abschreckung aufgeben,
> nur noch minimal flüstern, Bitteschön sagen . . .

> . . . when Uncle Dagobert again throws something new,
> the crackle and crunch machine
> and such-like all-purpose weapons Bang! on to the market
> till an hour later Whizzbuzz . . . Puff . . . Plop!
> conventional war, localized in the nursery,
> unorthodoxly flares up
> and our parents
> because the Christmas shopping
> permits only limited relaxation of tension
> and Huey, Dewey, and Louie, –
> those are Donald Duck's nephews, –
> for no reason have swapped shields and swords,
> give up their reciprocal, second
> and gradual deterrent, only
> minimally whisper now, and say please . . .

Moral judgement does not become explicit in this poem, and the
implicit judgement seems to be in favour of the children who plan a

family 'in which naughty is good and good naughty' rather than of the parents 'who everywhere stand around and talk of getting children and getting rid of children'. What is certain about the poem is that Grass's new realism has not denied him access to the imaginative freedom and verbal invention of his earlier work. About that realism – as evident in poems of personal experience like 'Ehe' ('Marriage') or 'Vom Rest unterm Nagel' ('Of the Residue under Our Nails') as in those touching on society and politics – there can be no doubt; and even in politics it is realism that Grass opposes to the utopianism of the left-wing and right-wing radicals.

Whatever Günter Grass may do next – and he is the most un-predictable of artists – his third book of poems points to a widening awareness; and this means that he is unlikely to take his realism and literalness beyond a certain point. His involvement in the practical business of politics has imposed a very perceptible strain on him, but his essentially unpuritanical temper has ensured that the creative tension between innocence and experience, spontaneity and self-discipline is always maintained. Another way of putting it is that, unlike the ideologists and radicals, Grass does not want to carry politics over into private life or into those artistic processes which have to do with personality. If *Ausgefragt* is dominated by public concerns, it also contains this short poem, 'Falsche Schönheit' ('Wrong Beauty'):

>Diese Stille,
>   also der abseits in sich verbissne Verkehr,
>   gefällt mir,
>und dieses Hammelkotelett,
>   wenn es auch kalt mittlerweile und talgig,
>   schmeckt mir,
>das Leben,
>   ich meine die Spanne seit gestern bis Montag früh,
>   macht wieder Spass:
>ich lache über Teltower Rübchen,
>unser Meerschweinchen erinnert mich rosa,
>Heiterkeit will meinen Tisch überschwemmen,
>und ein Gedanke,
>   immerhin ein Gedanke,
>   geht ohne Hefe auf;
>   und ich freue mich,
>   weil er falsch ist und schön.

This quiet,
   that is, the traffic some way off, its teeth stuck into itself,
     pleases me,
and this lamb cutlet,
   though cold by now and greasy,
     tastes good,
life,
   I mean the period from yesterday to Monday morning,
     is fun again:
I laugh at the dish of parsnips,
our guinea pig pinkly reminds me,
cheerfulness threatens to flood my table,
and an idea,
   an idea of sorts,
     rises without yeast;
      and I'm happy
        because it is wrong and beautiful.

Ideas that make one happy because they are 'wrong and beautiful' have no place in the austere post-Brechtian verse written by so many West and East German poets in the nineteen-sixties. When he wants to be, Grass can be as realistic as they are; but the court jester's freedom includes the right to be fantastic, playful and grotesque.

Grass's insistence on this freedom has a special importance against the background of a general crisis in West German literature, precipitated by its increasing politicization. While East German poets like Wolf Biermann and Reiner Kunze have been defending the individual against encroachments on his privacy on the part of an all-powerful collective, or of an all-powerful bureaucracy that claims to represent the collective, many West German writers have done their best to deprive themselves of such personal liberty as they enjoy. In extreme cases, like that of Hans Magnus Enzensberger, the conflict between social conscience and personal inclination has led to a virtual renunciation of imaginative writing. Those who have followed critical opinion in West Germany over the years will be familiar with statements about what can no longer be written: love poems, because love is a form of bourgeois self-indulgence; nature poems, because we live in a technological age; confessional poems, or poems of personal experience, because they are poems of personal experience; moon poems, because, as Peter Rühmkorf suggested well before the first moon landing, cosmonauts are better qualified to deal with the moon than poets. Needless to say, all those kinds of poems have continued to be written, even if they have been written in new ways. Yet the fact remains that a great many people have been busy restricting the range of poetry. To be fair to them, there is some truth in most of their arguments, and a certain excitement is generated by discoveries of what one can no longer do. What is dangerous is to be dogmatic about it or to persuade oneself that one mustn't write this or that kind of poem because it has become anachronistic. If all poetry is an anachronism – and it was felt to be that as long ago as the early stages of the Industrial Revolution – so is almost every other human activity and the human species itself. Günter Grass's court jester at a non-existent court is undoubtedly an anachronism; but perhaps it is wise at present not to be thrown into a panic by that word, since the more we panic, the more we accelerate the process of obsolescence.

Günter Grass, in any case, has not worried too much about what can and cannot be written, according to the latest theoretical appraisal of the state of civilization. He has written what he was impelled to write, with a prodigal energy which – even in poems – has involved the risk of error, of tactlessness, of 'wrong beauty', of bad taste. It remains to be seen whether Günter Grass can maintain his energy and spontaneity as a poet not only in the teeth of the ideological constrictors, to whom he has made no concessions, but also as he moves farther and farther away from childhood and the peculiar imaginative sources of his art. Since there is a limit to the fruitful tension between the politician and the clown, or between any kind of arduous practical involvement and the state of openness which poetry demands, it is my hope that conditions in Germany will soon make it unnecessary for Grass to assume responsibilities that ought to be borne by persons without his unique talents as a writer and artist. The tension, as I have tried to show, was there from the first, even when the clown seemed to have it all his way, and the moralist in Grass had not yet involved him in party politics. There is no reason why it should cease if my hope is fulfilled, since in poets practical experience is transmuted into awareness, and innocence is never lost, but renews itself within the awareness.

The Trouble with Francis*

POETS who feel the need to write autobiographies or memoirs, and
many do, come up against a tangle of difficulties. One is inherent in
this kind of writing and not peculiar to them. Autobiography is not
a form or a genre. It has no rules, conventions or precedents, other
than those imposed by libel laws. One can begin at the beginning, as
far as chronology goes – and chronology doesn't go far enough – but
one can't end at the end. As for the middle, it's the worst stretch of
all, the hardest to get into perspective, make sense of, keep interesting and alive. The usual way out is some sort of faking – a resort to
semi-fiction, dramatizing or mythologizing of one's outer life. Public
men can stuff the thing with public documents revealing as much as
they choose to reveal of what they did or failed to do in a particular
situation. Most poets, if they are honest, know that the public side
of their lives has little to do with the activity that distinguishes them,
the writing of poems; and what little they know about that they
usually like to keep to themselves. So they are left with the material
of which anyone's life is mainly made up – and literary reminiscences,
gossip, talking shop.

Robert Francis was so little talked and written about, at least in
England, that I might never have got to know his poetry if I hadn't
been taken to see him during my first short visit to America in 1965;
and to meet Robert Francis once, in his own setting, was an experience as distinct and unforgettable as to read his autobiography. It
was to get a sense of the totality of his life and work, for everything
about him and around him was of his own choosing, his own making.
Another happy chance brought me to the Connecticut valley for a
longer stay in the following year. The autobiography adds a wealth
of significant details to the acquaintance, but – despite the three
confessions it contains – my first impression of the man and the
poems remains unchanged. The book is as unassuming, as clear-cut

* *The Trouble with Francis* (An Autobiography), Robert Francis, Univ. of
Massachusetts Press, Amherst, 1971.

and as extraordinary as the person. For one thing, it doesn't fake, dramatize, mythologize or indulge in 'poetic' prose – that vulgar evasion of the true business of autobiography. For another, it can afford to do without those accretions, because, in his unique way, Robert Francis succeeded in combining 'perfection of the work' with 'perfection of the life'. Though a professional writer for most of his adult life, he became expert in the art of making a little go a long way, keeping out of what didn't concern him, cultivating his garden – even while circumstances forced him to work in other people's. His life, as he writes, has been one of 'fulfillment and control'.

With the exception of Robert Frost, a friend and mentor, hardly one famous writer makes a major appearance in the book – for the simple and adequate reason that none played a major part in Robert Francis's life. The only shocking confession in his book, as he points out himself, is what he calls his dislike of poetry:

> Much of it I detest. Yet over the years I have had to pretend, more or less, that what was giving me pain was giving me pleasure ... No wonder I have been reluctant to admit that the thing I have devoted my life to is a thing I usually want to flee from ... Why couldn't I think of a single poet I had any particular desire to meet? There is more than one answer to that question, but perhaps it is enough to say that to visit a poet is to put oneself at the mercy both of his poetry and of himself.

It takes a poet as truthful, and as roguish, as Robert Francis to admit that the urge to write one's own poems doesn't necessarily make one receptive to other people's, because one monomania – and to devote one's life to writing poetry is monomania – excludes another. The admission leaves Robert Francis free to concentrate on the real substance of his life, his discovery and practice of the virtue of frugality. This is what makes his book exemplary at a time when it's becoming clear that this earth can be ravaged and made uninhabitable without the help of nuclear bombs – by the exploitation and waste of its resources in the production race. Frugality means both economy and fruitfulness. By providing statistics of his income and expenditure, of the plants he grows and eats, of the things he buys and does not buy, Robert Francis shows how frugality can work in practice on the East Coast of the U.S.A., in 1970; and how its practice can lead to happiness, 'fulfillment and control'. His book ought to be read for that alone, and read by persons who have never come across a line of his poetry. They should read his poems, too, if they detest poetry less than he does, but the book is so far from being a 'literary auto-biography' in terms either of shop or self-analysis that its importance doesn't depend in the least on the importance or fame accorded to Robert Francis as a poet.

Not that Francis is a hot gospeller of frugality, or of any of the other virtues his autobiography embodies. As the ironic title announces – it is a quotation from a review of one of his books of poems – his sense of humour is as evident in the autobiography as his seriousness and his single-mindedness. One of Francis's roles, for a long time, has been that of 'the satirical rogue'. His book would be less persuasive if he had set out to convert others, instead of telling the story of how a timid and conventional man, the son of a Baptist minister, found his own way of life, his own way of being happy and his own view of the world – a pessimistic and agnostic one, Francis confesses, because of his deep concern with the sufferings of others and his awareness that suffering is inescapable. That it took him till late middle age to discover that he was homosexual shows what obstacles Francis had to overcome in his quest of personal happiness; and though the good life he has made for himself demands more solitude than most people are able to bear, his book is full of shrewd and sympathetic responses to relatives, neighbours and casual acquaintances whose occupations and needs were quite different from his.

Not the least distinction of *The Trouble with Francis* has to do with control as much as with fulfilment. Coolness is a word that has been very fashionable in professedly anti-conformist circles, but most of the writing produced and consumed by them has been chaotic, incoherent and hysterical. Both in his poems and his auto-biography Robert Francis has kept cool; not out of indifference or apathy, but a true serenity and balance attained by hard work, on his own terms. It is refreshing to read a book by a man who pities others more than he pities himself, who can get on with his work unstimulated by vanity, greed or competition, and who has learnt to find richness in what most people would call poverty.

George Oppen's
*Collected Poems**

THOUGH George Oppen's first book, *Discrete Series*, appeared nearly forty years ago, with a preface by Ezra Pound, his work has received little attention in this country; or in America, for that matter, at least until he received the Pulitzer Prize in 1969. Very few of the would-be representative anthologies include it at all, and the same is true of critical surveys. Specialists and students may know of Oppen as a member of the Objectivist group, but that group itself remained obscure for several decades, until the recent revival of interest in the work of Oppen, Charles Reznikoff, Carl Rakosi and, of course, Louis Zukofsky. Even now it is difficult for a non-specialist to find any critical comment on the practice of the group or movement as such, though William Carlos Williams's association with it has been fairly well documented.

Williams's 'No idea/but in things' might serve as a motto, but it could easily be a misleading one, if taken too literally as a programme or prescription. Carl Rakosi has written that the aim of Objectivism was

> to present objects in their essential reality and to make of each poem an object . . . meaning by this, obviously, the opposite of a subject; the opposite, that is, of all forms of *personal vagueness*, of loose bowels and streaming, sometimes screaming, consciousness. And how does one make into an object the subjective experience from which a poem issues? By feeling the experience sincerely, by discriminating particularity, by honesty and intelligence, by imagination and craftsmanship . . . qualities not belonging to Objectivists alone.

This definition is so close to many other prescriptions for good writing in our century that one is tempted to forget all about Objectivism in approaching the work of George Oppen, quite

* Fulcrum Press, London, 1972.

especially in view of the philosophical and psychological complexities inherent in Rakosi's object/subject antinomy.

Yet those very complexities are a real clue to George Oppen's constant preoccupations, and to the distinction of his work. The poems from his first collection – not followed by another until nearly thirty years later, in 1962 – are difficult precisely because they present objects, clusters of objects, situations, complex perceptions not linked by argument, narrative, or an easily recognizable subjective correlative. It is not till the second collection, *The Materials*, that what seemed like an alienation of subject from object is shown to have been a reciprocity, the process of perceiving a mode of self-discovery:

> What I've seen
> Is all I've found: myself

'Product'

or:

> And all I've been
> Is not myself? I think myself
> Is what I've seen and not myself

'Myself I Sing'

As this process of self-discovery continues, the manner becomes less elliptical, though Oppen's art remains one of extreme spareness. Paradoxically, this poet of clearly denoted phenomena – mechanical or architectural as often as natural or human – turns out to be a rigorous thinker about the relations between individuals and society, between consciousness and environment – about 'the world, weather-swept, with which one shares the century', to quote from the very first poem in the book. Complex interactions and relationships are his theme; whether between father and child, as in 'From a Photograph', or between a man and a particular urban scene, which in turn becomes 'the realm of nations', as in 'Time of the Missile'. If this suggests only austerity and tough-mindedness, at which Oppen does excel, readers should turn to the poem 'Psalm' (p. 60), a celebration of seeing deer, or of the tenderness and wonderment of the seeing ('That they are there!'). 'The Bicycles and the Apex', from the same collection of 1965, enacts a response quite as intense to the 'mechanisms . . . Light/And miraculous' that have become

> Part of the platitude
> Of our discontent.

One thing that Oppen owes to his early objectivist discipline is that in his poems social criticism of America is inseparable from personal or confessional lyricism. He does not need to protest, rant, howl or ironize. The social criticism is as completely merged in the objects he presents as any other element of experience or response.

> I have not and never did have any motive of poetry
> But to achieve clarity

he writes in a late poem sequence, 'Route'; but the clarity he achieves is never simplistic or banal, because of the subtlety of his thought and sensibility, his concern with the discrepancies between individual and collective awareness ('There is madness in the number/Of the living'), and his grappling with the metaphysical complexities already mentioned:

> Reality, blind eye
> Which has taught us to stare.

As an instance of the spareness, clarity, and the increasing direct-ness with which Oppen has rendered delicate perceptions (no longer necessarily visual) I want to quote one complete poem, 'A Barbarity', from his latest collection, *Seascape: Needle's Eye*:

> We lead our real lives
> in dreams
> one said meaning
> because he was awake
> we are locked in ourselves
> That was not what he dreamed
> in any dream
> he dreamed the weird morning
> of the bird waking.

This latest collection, by the way, was published separately by The Sumac Press (Fremont, Michigan) in 1972. The poem 'The Song' in *Collected Poems* (p. 157) appears there in a longer version as 'Song, the Winds of Downhill'; and the Sumac book contains a number of sea poems not included in the *Collected Poems*.

George Oppen strikes me as a poet who has come through by the hardest way, resisting facile effects and comfortable epiphanies. Every line in his book has been wrung from recalcitrant realities, by outstaring the 'blind eye'. In 'To C.T.', originally part of a letter to

Charles Tomlinson, divided into lines at his suggestion, Oppen writes: 'One imagines himself/addressing his peers/I suppose. Surely/that might be the definition/of "seriousness"?' It is; but it is also the definition of work that is worth reading and re-reading by persons who don't think of themselves as the poet's peers.